Praise for Moving Moments

Moving Moments is the second offering by Karen Lang, and within its pages, the reader will again find the gift of her gentle, compassionate wisdom. Having experienced tragically losing her 9-year-old son Nathan twenty years ago, this volume will undoubtedly speak directly to the hearts and minds of those living with grief. Yet *Moving Movements* has lessons for us all. It provides practical guidance to support the reader in creating a quiet, still space for silence as well as nurturing a curiosity of self. With Karen's tender yet probing questions as a guide, we are asked to turn inwards and unpack our past and present motivations as well as future intentions. *Moving Movements* is the ultimate guide for holding an internal dialogue with Karen, equipping the reader with the background necessary for each question, while providing all the tools for any encountered scenario. Despite the universality of the grief experience, and as a community unaccustomed to interrogating same, Karen's book is for anyone needing direction to navigate the oft fraught complexity of modern living.

Alyson Gundry, Bachelor of Social Work (Hons)
Graduate Certificate in Bereavement Counselling and Intervention / Paediatric Palliative Care Services / Children's Health Queensland Hospital

Moving Moments is a very personal story about the wisdom Karen has gained from facing her grief. Unlike other stories of loss, this unique book of hope offers the reader practical ways to navigate and move through the dark valleys of their suffering and up into the mountains of their potential. Karen's story is medicine for the soul and a pathway to our freedom.

Illundi, Ancestral Healer, Sydney, Australia

In *Moving Moments*, Karen Lang shares with us both her experience of grieving the loss of her son, and the powerful, transformative lessons and tools she learned and developed as she went through her grieving and healing process. In addition, at the end of each chapter, the author provides the reader with 'Questions to ask in Stillness', that is, tools for the reader to do their own introspective, emotional healing, and spiritually transformative work. There is also a chapter specifically on meditation exercises for furthering our personal growth. *Moving Moments* is both moving and inspirational, and I would recommend it to my spiritual counselling clients in a heartbeat.

Julianne Victoria, Spiritual Counsellor & Author,
California, USA

Moving Moments begins with a devastating reality. Death and grief. The name of the book itself should not be underestimated, however, because the answers to many of life's questions can be found here. Death breaks into our lives like a thief and often when we are completely unprepared. Death robs us of those we hold dear, and we feel lost when it comes to coping with its aftermath. As each page delicately reveals, Karen has a great desire to give the reader useful tools to deal with suffering. Karen not only gives the reader effective strategies for life but shares who she has become despite her devastating loss.

Oana Cercel, Italy

MOVING MOMENTS

TRANSFORM YOUR SUFFERING
INTO FREEDOM

KAREN LANG

Published in Queensland, Australia

Copyright © 2021 by Karen Lang

All rights reserved. Apart from fair dealing for the purposes of study, research, criticism or review as permitted under the Copyright Act, no part of this publication may be reproduced, distributed or transmitted in any form or by any means without prior written permission.

The information in this book is not intended to replace professional medical or psychological advice. The content is based upon the author's personal and professional experiences, opinions and qualifications.

All necessary written permissions have been obtained from clients to publish their individual stories. Names have been changed to protect their identities. Other written permissions have been obtained for quoted material. Epigraphs and poems are the intellectual property of the author.

Karen Lang: www.karenlangauthor.com

Cover design by Judith San Nicolas
Typeset in Perpetua 9/12 & 22pt
Printed and bound in Australia by IngramSpark
Prepared for publication by Dr Juliette Lachemeier @ The Erudite Pen

A catalogue record for this book is available from the National Library of Australia

Moving Moments: Transform your suffering into freedom – Karen Lang, first ed.
ISBN 978-0-6452015-0-5(paperback)
ISBN 978-0-6452015-1-2 (eBook)

I am here
present
in this moving moment
where everything is felt
where everything is seen
where life is both full and empty
and where all possibilities live.

Karen Lang

Dedication

This book is dedicated to my three beautiful children, Nathan, Lauren and April. They continually teach me how precious and abundant each moment is and always show me the meaning of love and how to embrace its power.

Contents

Preface i

Introduction v

Part One—Moving Moments

The Moment My Life Changed 1

Rising from the Ashes 5

Moments of Forgiveness 17

Moments of Surrender 25

Moments of Oneness 31

Part Two—Everything is Felt

Moments of Stillness and Movement 43

Moments of Darkness 51

Moments of Judgement 57

Moments of Anxiety 67

Moments of Anxiety in our Children 75

Moments in Nature 81

Ancestral Healing 87

Moments of Truth 99

Part Three—Everything is Seen

Our Hidden Treasure 109

Responsibility 115
Universal Languages...................................... 123
Our Health.. 127
Moments of Resilience.................................. 137

Part Four—Possibilities

Gateway to our Senses................................... 143
Sacred Moments 149
Dreaming Moments 155
Goal Setting... 161
A Simple Life 167
Meditations — Stillness & Movement................. 175
Final Thoughts... 193
Acknowledgements 197
Further Reading... 199
Notes.. 201

Preface

Life is made up of moving moments; we are either moving through them or we are being moved by them.

There are touching moments, a-ha moments, joyful moments, silent moments, tragic moments and end-of-life moments. In a moment, everything can change. In a moment, we can be left with nothing. In a moment, we can be moved to find our true purpose in life.

No matter who we are, we are the sum of all our moments.

Like ice melting in our hand, each moment is fleeting, but its memory can last a lifetime. However, we cannot live in the fullness of each moment or move through life easily while we hold on to past traumas or emotional wounds. In Celtic tradition, which is my heritage, time is depicted as a wheel that is always turning and moving through the cycles of life.

In my first book, *Courage*, I share details about my life leading up to my nine-year-old son's death in 2001 and how I learned to cope after he was hit by a car and killed. In *Courage*, I took readers step by step through my grief and offered strategies and practices to cope with the loss of a loved one.

In *Moving Moments*, my second book, I take the reader on a deeper journey into my spiritual life and share the insights and wisdom I have discovered since 2001. As an energy healer and intuitive life coach, I share my own personal stories, epigraphs, poems and spiritual metaphors. I also share permissible client case studies (names changed to protect identities). These provide examples of the limiting stories and beliefs we all hold onto. Throughout the book, I question these beliefs and offer strategies and practices that will awaken our authentic nature. I share how we can keep moving with life instead of clinging to the past and our suffering.

When I faced my son's death, I also faced my past and how I had lived. I became aware of all the moments I had missed and felt the guilt and regrets that came with it. From this place, I had a choice: to move with life and expand my authentic self or to become a victim of my past.

My son's death was a wakeup call to my reality and an opportunity to live more fully in my truth. Once I committed to this and moved into a relationship with spirit, nature and life, I experienced a profound rebirth and a new way of being. I awakened parts of myself that I had not seen before and began a lifelong journey of healing.

I hope this book inspires you and encourages you to move through your own suffering and into the fullness of each moment. In sharing my experiences, may you awaken the ancient wisdom you carry in your DNA and see all the beauty, courage and love you have within. May you see there is no separation in life and remember you are connected to everything. When you align with this truth, it will always guide you onto pathways that expand and support you. The decision to trust in this is the beginning of all wisdom and the door to your freedom.

Introduction

If you take the time to be still in nature, the first thing you will notice is the harmonious and constant flow of moving moments. Over time, it's like watching an orchestrated symphony that changes each day.

As you sit quietly, you will become aware of the steady and constant movement of the clouds. The soft sway of the trees. The easy flow of the river. The background harmony and melody of sounds. The sporadic movement of bird and animal life.

However, if you sit for a little longer, you will begin to feel what is not harmonious in you. You will feel the urgency to move. You will feel the insistent need to listen to your busy thoughts and their constant chatter. Sit a little longer and you will feel your fears, your sadness, or a deep anger you buried years ago.

There is a saying: *Allow your feelings to move and change in stillness, or they will eventually move and change you.* My story gives you the tools and strategies to do this. My book will guide you to feel, move and understand these feelings, and will open and awaken what is intuitive, beautiful and light in you. Over time, you will move and flow with the symphony of life.

Part One—Moving Moments

The Moment My Life Changed

In the end, the only thing that matters is how much we loved.

After the tragic shock and chaos of watching my nine-year-old son Nathan being hit by a car in 2001, my husband and I sat in the intensive care unit, amazed at how life went on without us. Although nothing had changed for anyone else, I was in the hospital, praying that my son's head injuries, after being thrown into the air by the force of the car, would not be fatal.

Time stopped as I sat by Nathan's bedside. He was fully sedated and placed on life support in the hope that his brain swelling would settle over a day or so. The results from the CAT scan were not good. His skull had been crushed after being hit by the car, and our only hope was to reduce the swelling.

I focused on every machine he was attached to and watched for any slight changes or signs that he was responding. With tears in our eyes, each time a doctor or nurse came near us, my husband and I hoped for a positive response.

Apart from a small cut on his leg, Nathan looked completely normal. There were no broken bones, stitches or bruises. All the injuries were in his skull and brain stem. The brain stem controls the flow of messages between the brain and the rest of the body, and it controls basic body functions such as breathing, swallowing, heart rate, blood pressure and consciousness.

The ICU became our home for the next few days. We roamed the hospital corridors in shock, crying and comforting one another. On the first night, I wept quietly with my dad, trying to make sense of everything that had happened. After a while, we both realised there were no words or explanations. Feeling his compassion and love in the silence was exactly what I needed in that moment.

The next day, having survived on only a few minutes of sleep, I began to feel overwhelmed and anxious. A neurologist came into test Nathan's brainwaves and breathing by turning off his ventilator. The doctor said that if he failed to breathe unsupported, he would be declared brain dead.

The silence was deafening as I willed my son to breathe on his own.

The test only took a few moments, but it was agonising to watch. I held my breath, too scared to let go. I begged Nathan to fight harder and urged him to gasp for air. In the end, I turned away. The doctor reattached his ventilator. I felt numb, knowing what this meant.

Shortly afterwards, the head doctor of intensive care invited my husband and me to a private room for a meeting. I remember her shutting the door, making the room feel smaller than it already was. By the look on her face, we knew deep down what she was about to say and yet, in those dark hours, we still held on to hope.

The doctor looked tired as she explained that the irreversible damage to Nathan's brain stem from his skull being crushed on the road had left him brain dead. She explained that we could keep him on life support if we wished; however, at some point his heart would become overloaded and finally stop. She couldn't say when.

Hesitatingly, she told us that the alternative was to say our last goodbyes and donate his organs. We nodded in disbelief, too scared to open our mouths in case screams of agony escaped. Standing up to leave, I wondered how I would find the strength to share this news with family and friends. I wondered how anyone coped after hearing this.

My husband and I walked back to Nathan's bedside, wanting to just take him home and pretend that nothing had happened. We closed the door and sat next to his lifeless body, praying that no one else would walk in to share more information about his impending death.

We held him and kissed his precious face as our tears overflowed. Questions flooded my mind like, 'How could he be so vibrant and active just a day ago and now be on life support?'

Our last moments with Nathan were devastating. Knowing we would not hold him again or watch him grow up was unbearable. We did not want to imagine a life without him and could not understand how anyone survived the death of child. [1]

Rising from the Ashes

Rising from the ashes requires us to dig deep, find our courage and face the fire of grief.

When I first faced my grief, it consumed me. At its core, I felt lost and overwhelmed, and believed that my only escape was to run from its flames. And yet, as I cautiously moved towards grief and learned from it, I began to rise from the ashes like a phoenix and awaken my deepest sense of self.

I learned that grief was not just my feelings of loss but a skill to learn, like a new language. And like any new language, my first reaction was to try and understand it with my mind. But grief cannot be understood by the intellect of the mind. The language of grief demands it be felt by the heart.

Grief was far from simple, and its meaning refused to be limited to sorrow and suffering. Deeply confused by its presence each day, and because no one in my community had ever faced the death of a child before, I realised that grief was a complex, multidimensional journey to live through. Initially I felt fear and apprehension, but as time moved on, I understood that my only relief from its demands was to become intimate with it.

Grief stripped away my ego, old stories and beliefs. It revealed the shaky ground I had lived on and exposed my fears, like a lion standing over a mouse. Grief taught me that the more I acknowledged my feelings, the lighter I felt. Over time, I began to trust in this and build a new foundation to stand on.

Author and teacher, Stephen Jenkinson says, 'Grief is not a feeling, it is a capacity. It is not something that disables you, we are not on the receiving end of grief, we are on the practising end of grief.'[2]

Grief informed me and awakened me to the fragility and impermanence of life. These were not insights or wisdom I was aware of before my son's death. As a student of grief, my practice each day was to learn how to nurture the feelings that grief revealed to me. Over time, grief opened my capacity to forgive, to heal and to love myself more deeply.

I understood that when I didn't allow myself to go beyond the surface of my grief and enter the dark vulnerable spaces in me, I missed valuable lessons and opportunities to heal.

In becoming intimate with grief, there were days when I felt like I could not breathe or trust there was a reason to live, and on those days, I wept deeply for my son and for all the moments with him that were now lost. I learned to surrender in these moments and forgive myself. In this vulnerable space, I nestled deeply into the cave of darkness, away from life and the lure to quick-fix my suffering.

I did not always find meaning in those moments but rather an awakening and a willingness to move with the rise and fall of my breath. I understood that in order to heal, I had to accept both the dark and the light equally.

Everything we run away from, like our fears or our dark feelings of grief, will defeat us in the end. Death and grief became my teachers of life. However, when I did not respond to its call to move beyond my fears and back into the fullness of life, I was led onto pathways that were challenging and difficult.

Often clients will say to me, 'I cannot face my overwhelming feelings of grief' or 'If I allow myself to feel, I will fall apart'. This is not true. In fact, our capacity to feel is infinite, and with support and guidance, each of us holds the strength to do this again and again. However, our capacity to ignore our feelings or try to work things out in our mind is limited and can lead to emotional health issues.

Grief encouraged me to open my heart and helped me discover my authentic truth. It asked me to heal the parts of me that felt lost and separated. It asked me to face my insecurities, my people-pleasing habits and my limiting thoughts. As I moved through this understanding, I was slowly led into a reunion with life.

In the end, I had to choose how to live each day: face my emotions and my fears of the future, or stay in the grave with my son.

So how did I learn to understand the language of grief? I was changed forever after Nathan's death. I learned the hard way that to fully integrate the experience and understand the steps towards healing, I had to surrender everything I had previously learned or believed about life and myself.

Growing up, we may have learned to fear death or believe that if we move quickly enough and control life, death will not find us. Most of us were not taught how to prepare for death or how to honour those who have passed. Many of us did not grow up learning meaningful rituals and ceremonies that not only move and heal our grief, but connect us to life more deeply.

Many of our ancestors practised beautiful ceremonies and rituals for the dead. They placed high value on immortality and believed that the preservation of their memory created a deep purpose in life. They honoured those who had died with songs and poems, called elegies, that were sung to honour and grieve their loved ones.

Over time, the influence of busyness and technology has slowly separated us from this knowledge and understanding. However, this ancestral wisdom still lives within our DNA, and each of us has an opportunity to awaken this wisdom and to re-connect to the sacred.

Growing up, death was something we never spoke about in my family. It was never a conversation our generation thought was important. I learned that the depth of my grief was a reflection of how well I believed I had loved. Playing out like an old movie, I saw how many times I had taken my life and my son's life for granted. I saw the many times I was too busy or had lived unconsciously. Death showed me how much I had missed and the choices I had made along the way. Now, all I could do was sit and feel this painful truth until I had the courage to forgive myself.

Longing for the physical presence of those who have died, especially a child, is a difficult transition to move through. It took many years for me to understand that at some point I needed to let go of my physical relationship with Nathan and learn to accept my new relationship with Nathan in spirit.

Our family took our time to let go of his clothes, his toys and his books. Each time we did, we allowed a space for our new reality to sink in and to trust we could survive this deep change. While there is no rush to do this, I do believe it is important to set a timeframe around letting go of some of our loved one's possessions so we can create room for new a relationship with life.

While family and friends might call these belongings unimportant, for those who grieve, these items represent experiences, memories and the last thread left to prove their child or loved one existed. This is a difficult time of surrender and letting go, but we must trust we have the courage and resilience to step into the unknown and heal over time.

Another reason it may seem difficult to let go of these items is because grief takes up so much of our energy and having to decide what to keep or to give away can feel overwhelming. And so, this is a good time to ask our family and friends for support and to gain a different perspective in this situation.

Sometimes during my grief, family and friends did not feel comfortable around my sadness, confusion or anger; however, over time, I learned that grieving is not a time to worry about how others are feeling or how they were making me feel. I realised it needed to be a sacred and patient time to focus on my own needs and how to survive. At times it was messy, complicated and overwhelming, but when I gave myself the space to feel this, I found relief and a growing trust that I could move through it.

I learned that being in nature taught me to slow down my thoughts and find clarity in my suffering. I saw that in nature everything dies for a time before it returns in a new form. I began to understand that I needed to be patient as I returned to life in a new way and into a new future without my son.

I began with a yoga class to calm my busy mind.

Afterwards, I noticed how this calmed my energy, and I began to sleep more soundly. Over time, I was led to a spiritual healer who guided and supported me to see life from a new perspective. She taught me how to begin a practice of ceremony and meditation. And even though I struggled and felt hopeless at times, I committed to a practice of stillness and listening, and discovered this was the steppingstone to my freedom. In the dark spaces of letting go, I took the steps towards a beautiful transformation and was moved by the beauty and support of life.

From here, I began a daily practice of stillness and movement: movement in my yoga classes, breathwork and walking, and stillness in my meditation, time in nature and listening. These practices allowed me to remember what is light and beautiful in me and became the foundation of my balance and presence. Each new day offers me a choice, to begin again and align with an infinite source of love.

Once I began to accept the death of my son and moved with the reality that came with it, I allowed my vulnerabilities and fears to be felt and seen. I began to see that the intensity of my grief would not end if I kept hoping at some point that things would return to normal. I realised that my life in the present moment was my 'new normal' and although this was distressing at times, I understood that dying to my old ways of being was the answer.

Over time, I felt a new strength arise in me. I learned that each time I stepped out and faced the fire of grief, or the unknown, resilience awakened within.

I understood that it was the courage to face my fears that earned me the right to step into my power.

I think that universally we have forgotten our deep capacity not only to move through grief but to transform from it. Instead of focusing on the gateway of resilience and expansion in grief, often we are taught to focus on what we cannot cope with, or what people insist we cannot do after the death of a loved one. In doing so, we forget the power of the lion that lays dormant within each of us and arises each time we step into our courage.

I realised I had faced and survived one of the most difficult things a parent can do. I had buried my child. This is something I need to acknowledge and honour. This is true courage and strength, and if I can bury my child, anything is possible.

We can trust that we have all the strength we need to handle every situation in life and that our fearless determination will arise when we need it the most.

Rising from the ashes does not happen once, but many times in our life. Trust that each of us holds a blueprint within that allows a creative and unique response to life. We just need to give ourselves space to discover what that is and to receive the right support along the way.

Life is always changing and evolving and when we move with it and stop resisting, we will find freedom from our suffering.

Once my practice was established, I slowly felt a new perspective emerge. On the days when uncertainty or fear still take over, I go inward to nurture these feelings. In special moments, I feel 'one' with the universe and feel its deep love, support and compassion.

Being with our loved ones before death

Another sacred and difficult space to live through is being present with our loved ones before they pass. Often when I speak to people who work with the dying or who have been with someone before they pass, they share that it is common for adults and children not to speak about their upcoming death. Sometimes this is because it feels too confronting, or because their fears of the unknown are too difficult to articulate with another.

Having time with a loved one before they pass is a precious and sacred time, and I had this experience with my beautiful friend Jean. She had been a lifelong friend of mine who battled with breast cancer for many years before the cancer spread to her lungs and sadly, she passed in June 2019.

Towards the end, she often felt too weak to have visitors; however, there was one morning where she felt stronger, and myself and two of her close friends took the opportunity to visit her in the hospital.

Jean was such a positive and generous woman throughout life. During her last few weeks, it was clear she did not want to speak about her death, so we respected this, and instead we nurtured her while we were with her. One friend gently brushed her hair while I massaged her feet, and our other friend massaged her hands.

It was beautiful to watch her receive our love and to be with her in her last moments. Friends for many years, we laughed and shared many stories together that day. As we hugged her gently and told her how much we loved her, we thought we had more time. However, the following day one of her sons called to announce she had passed.

Finding creative ways to respond to those who are about to pass only happens when we take the time to watch and wait for the signs they give. When we do this, it can lead us to spaces where everyone can feel safe to be vulnerable. A beautiful example of this deep listening is shared by a chaplain who was working with a patient at the end of her life.

As he spent time with her, he noticed how much she liked it when he rang the meditation bell. He asked her why she like the bell so much and she told him that she wanted to practise listening to the sound of the bell fading out. The chaplain took this as a cue and a way for this patient to express her feelings about death.

He would ask, 'What do you think it will be like when the bell fades out?' or 'Would you like to hear the bell today?' The chaplain shared how this allowed him to speak to this woman about death without her being confronted by it. The chaplain and the patient gently spoke together about the bell and where the sound of the bell would go. I love this simple and creative approach. Being with our loved ones before they pass need not be complicated or demanding. We just need to give them room to feel safe and nurtured and this will make all the difference.

After our loved ones have passed, we may feel guilty that we did not get to say what we wanted or that there wasn't an appropriate time or pause to express our love, forgiveness or gratitude. However, what I found during my time with Jean was how important it was to listen to what she needed rather than what I wanted to say or felt needed to be said between us.

I advise everyone to trust that if there is not a space to say what is needed, do not lose hope because we can speak to our loved ones freely after they have passed. It is just as effective in spirit as it is in person.

Questions to ask in Stillness

When we lose a loved one, we can feel uprooted and abandoned; however, over time, we must learn how to re-plant ourselves and be patient as we learn to grow in a new direction. During times of grief, often we are afraid to let go because we believe we will not cope or be able to handle our overwhelming feelings, but this is not true. When we suppress our feelings, they build up in our body and over time can lead to an anxiety attacks, angry outbursts or a lowered immune system.

Find a quiet place to sit with your journal and ask yourself the following questions. You may like to draw or paint any associated feelings that arise:

Who have I become in the wilderness of my grief?
Am I fearful? Angry? Do I feel lost?
What am I unwilling to feel and why?
Where do I feel separated or unsupported in life?
What regrets or guilt am I holding onto?
Do I need to ask for support and guidance?
How am I nurturing my grief and my energy each day?
Am I open to learning this new language of grief, step by step?
Do I believe I have the courage to face this journey?

Moments of Forgiveness

Learn from your mistakes and find freedom from forgiveness.

There were times after my son's death that I felt a deep satisfaction in my bitterness towards the driver who hit him. In difficult moments, I believed my anger was a righteous anger, and perhaps one that even Jesus would approve of.

Studies have shown that when people stay angry about the past or remain focused on someone who has hurt them, it lowers their vibration and energy. Over time, this energy becomes blocked. By staying angry, we can unconsciously carry the physiological symptoms of stress, which can cause physical problems and emotional outbursts.

However, letting go of these traumas and painful memories can seem impossible for some people. In my book *Courage*, I share how I forgave the driver and how angry I was before I made this decision. To begin the process of forgiveness, we must first accept and validate our feelings of anger, resentment or fear.

It is okay to feel angry and overwhelmed about our situation or want to separate from someone who has deeply hurt us or changed our life. Unforgiveness is a bitter emotion, but so are the despicable acts of suffering that people can cause one another.

As an energy healer, I have found it's normal for people to struggle with forgiveness. Often the reason we hold on to our anger is simply to take back some sense of control when we feel there is none. It's also a way we can hold on to the injustices that have been done to us that have yet not been punished.

However, holding on to our anger and suffering keeps us trapped in a karmic prison, and in this prison of pain, we can end up making the same decisions that we vowed we would never do. In this space, we never feel connected to the fullness of life and as we continue to hold onto our injustices, we become a magnet for those who have had the same experiences.

After my son's death, I found it extremely difficult to forgive myself and to let go of the guilt I carried. The night before my son died, he asked me to lay with him after he had gone to bed, but I was exhausted from work that day so I said no. That memory haunted me for years after his death, and at times, I felt overwhelmed that I had not been there for him.

Carrying guilt and punishing ourselves in this way can create unnecessary suffering, and the way to release this is to forgive ourselves.

It was several years later before I realised the toll this story was having on me and the suffering it was causing me. Together with my sister, I allowed room to release my guilt. Energetically it felt like I was carrying a heavy backpack on my shoulders, and I knew it was time to let it go. We cried together as I forgave myself. I forgave myself for all the times I had let my son down, real or imagined, and for the times I had let myself down, real or imagined. And as I breathed this out back into the earth, I instantly felt relief from this burden of guilt.

When we forgive and let go of our anger, resentment, guilt and fear, we create room for movement. This opens up new pathways to understand our oneness with life. It also awakens compassion in us and offers us freedom and unity rather than separation and suffering.

In the end, we can convince ourselves of all the reasons that unforgiveness is justified; however, when we hold on to unforgiveness, we also hold onto the emotional memories of it. Unfortunately, we cannot have one without the other, so if we do not forgive the person who has hurt us, we cannot release the emotional trauma we are holding in our body's memory.

An analogy to understand unforgiveness is to visualise the weeds in our garden. They can be unsightly and problematic at times but if we take the time to remove the weeds as they sprout, they are easy to control.

However, when we let the weeds grow, or ignore them altogether, then over time these weeds begin to spread. Eventually, they take over the flowers, the plants, the grass and the garden, and at this stage it feels impossible to change the situation or to deal with it.

And so, forgiveness is like weeding the garden. We are human, and we all make mistakes. We have hurt people, and people have hurt us. What matters the most is how we respond to these experiences.

I have learned that when I feel irritated or have been hurt by someone, I respond to these emotions as they arise, like the weeds in the garden. However, when I hold on to my resentment for another, I am not only planting weeds in my garden, but taking on their weeds as well.

It is also important to remember that when we continue to keep these weeds in our garden out of stubbornness or anger, they will continue to move down our family tree, and our children and their children will carry these weeds and have to deal with them in the future.

The more we forgive and let go, the more space we create for beautiful fruits of abundance. In doing this, we will see the humanness in each other and remember that we all make mistakes.

Of course, it requires discipline to deal with the weeds as they arise, but when we ignore our feelings, the weeds grow quietly in the background. Sometimes it's not until a physical illness or mental health issue arises that we discover our emotions and weeds have taken over our entire life.

In this place of overwhelm, I teach others to be patient and kind to themselves and to allow small steps of change. Over time, each of us will begin to see more flowers bloom.

Do not underestimate the affects that unforgiveness has on our body, energy and mind. In letting go, forgiveness is the very thing that releases us from future pain and suffering, and this allows us to move freely into every experience.

Stillness and Reflection Practice for Forgiveness

To forgive another
Find a quiet place either outside in nature or inside. Take some deep breaths in and out. Relax your body and trust you have the courage to do this. Ask your healthy ancestors, guides and angels to be with you.
Place your hand on your heart and say:
'I forgive (name) for all the harm you have caused me.
I forgive you for the pain and suffering you have created in my life.
Today I release this story I have carried for both of us.
Today I release this wound of suffering in me and I let it go.'
Breathe in and out three times to release this unforgiveness within.
Open your arms and say:
'Today I create room within to receive the love and abundance I deserve.'
Stay in this quiet space and receive until you are ready to finish.

Karen Lang

To forgive yourself
Find a quiet place either outside in nature or inside. Take some deep breaths in and out. Relax your body and trust you have the courage to do this. Ask your healthy ancestors, guides and angels to be with you.
Place your hand on your heart and say:
'I forgive myself for any harm I have done to myself or another.
Today I release the stories of guilt, anger, or judgement that I have carried within.
Today I release this wound of suffering in me and let it go.'
Breathe in and out three times to release this unforgiveness within.
Open your arms and say:
'Today I create room within to receive the love and abundance I deserve.'
Stay in this quiet space and receive until you are ready to finish.

Moments of Forgiveness

*

In life, I dance between light and shadow.
In the shadow, I see my old stories,
my scarcity and separateness.
And so, on days like these, I sit in stillness, allowing these
shadows to be felt, and I breathe them out.
In doing so, I begin to see the light moving around me again,
beckoning me to join in the dance of life.

Moments of Surrender

Surrender to the unknown and the whole universe will surrender to you.

I remember in my darkest days of grief when even breathing seemed difficult. When I was torn between not wanting to live so I could be with my son, and wanting to live as I watched my five-year-old daughter search for strength and courage in me.

It was a vulnerable and fragile space to be in, and I came in and out of it many times. Surrender was the space where I faced my fears of uncertainty. It was a place where only raw honesty could live.

Surrendering gave me an opportunity to move out of my limiting stories and into my heart space to receive. And although I felt naked and exposed, I focused on my breath and moved with it slowly. I focused on my purpose to live and to be here in each moment. From here, I slowly began to remember and awaken my ability to survive. I remembered I was more than the mistakes I had made. I was more than my past or the guilt I had carried. I realised that although I felt broken, I also felt a strength rise in me and a belief I could move through this.

I discovered that surrendering is not weak. Instead, I learned it takes great courage to be vulnerable and to admit I need help. I understood over time that I was responsible for changing my situation.

Life encourages us to avoid surrendering. We are told to soldier on, suck it up or just move on. Most of us have spent our entire lives creating and controlling our work schedules, our home life, our food, our social life and our children, but grief and suffering will not tolerate the illusion of control.

Surrendering is simply allowing and moving with each moment as it is. No matter how desperate we may feel, or what is happening around us, we need to trust we can face it all. It means moving with the ever-changing landscape of life and understanding that even if today was a great, tomorrow is not guaranteed.

Surrender is often linked to words like 'letting go' or 'going with the flow'. But to me, surrendering is far more complex. Surrendering is a death of self and our old belief system. It is letting go of how we expected life to turn out and accepting the journey we have been given. It is a daily practice of stepping into the unknown and discovering our deepest potential.

Surrendering begins the moment we realise that everything we have tried to control or attempted to do has failed. It's the last stop at the station, the final straw, and until we arrive here, we are not surrendering.

Moments of Forgiveness

When Nathan died, a part of me awakened for the first time. The moment he became unconscious, I became conscious of the illusions I had been living and the false identities I had played out for others. It was painful, messy and complicated; however, it was also an opportunity for me to wake up and see a deeper perspective and purpose in life.

Running away or distracting ourselves from this truth may seem easier at the time. Nevertheless, our suffering and pain will not pass until we are ready to face it. Surrendering invites us to dig deeper. To let go of our ego and pride and trust we will be supported as we move through life.

Sadhguru, an Indian author, spiritual teacher and Yogi, shares a metaphor about surrender. He compares our suffering to being trapped in a prison, and although it appears we can never leave this prison of suffering, there is, however, a pathway to our freedom. The way out of this prison and the limitations we have created is through the gutter of surrender.

It is a filthy, slimy, dark gutter and is not something any one would choose willingly, but it is the only way out. It is a lonely and dark place to be in, and at times, words are powerless to describe how we feel. In this space we must surrender everything we have known and learn to adapt to our new environment. And although the filth will get up our nose, in our mouth and over every part of our body, it will not matter – because with strong conviction, we will know this is the pathway to freedom.

Sadhguru describes surrender as the realisation that we cannot sustain our current form or experience for another moment – and so, we choose.[3]

Questions to ask in Stillness

Find a quiet place to sit with your journal and ask yourself the following questions. You may like to draw or paint any associated feelings that arise:

Am I ready to surrender?
Am I ready to be honest and authentic about the situation I am in?
Am I ready to take responsibility for my past and heal over time?
Can I allow others to support me and guide me out of the prison I am in?
Can I be vulnerable with others and listen to the truth?
Can I allow myself to be nurtured and receive what I need?

Moments of Forgiveness

*

For us to learn
We must let go of our need to be right.
For us to let go of our busyness
We must learn to become still.
For us to learn our truth
We must surrender our control.
For us to heal
We must admit we are sick.
For us to live fully
We must accept that we will die.

Moments of Oneness

When we understand we are 'one' with everyone and everything, we will find peace.

As I mentioned in chapter three, after my son's death, I initially began to blame, judge and feel a deep anger towards the driver. Instead of feeling my overwhelming emotions, it felt easier to direct my energy into blame and justice.

I saw the driver as someone who was separate from me. I saw nothing in the driver that was in me, nor did I have any intention of changing that. I wanted her to suffer as much as I was. Looking back, I can see how people stay trapped in this place of blame, judgement and separation after someone has hurt or killed their loved one.

At that time, it became easier for me to stay in a space of separation and convince myself that I was the victim and the driver was the enemy. However, when I separated myself from the driver, I separated from our shared fragility and vulnerability. I separated from my compassion and my ability to forgive. I separated from peace and an opportunity to see the truth.

In separation, I suffered just as much as the driver.

As I began to step towards the long journey of acknowledging my deepest, darkest feelings and the trauma I had faced, I found this separation in me. I found judgement in me. I found a deep sadness and grief in me. Discovering this part of me allowed me to see the driver for the first time.

I saw she was a mother, just like me. I recognised she was hurting, just like me. I saw the toll that my son's death had had on her and her family, just like me. I saw the unforgiveness she was holding for herself, and I saw the unforgiveness I was holding towards her.

For the first time, I saw her humanness. I saw the tragic mistake she had made. I saw the many times I had made mistakes, and I saw the many times I was not present in life. When I recognised this separation in me, I was moved, and I began to feel compassion and a common space between us. This discovery gave me the courage to forgive the driver and begin my path towards healing.

As a universal oneness awakened in me, I learned there was a deeper connection to life than the one I was experiencing. I recognised my shared humanity, common problems and common imperfections. I began to feel more compassion and patience for those I worked with and met, and I recognised we were all wounded in some way.

Understanding why we want to separate from another person is the first step. I have found this usually occurs when the people we are with or the experience we are having awakens a painful memory or a rejected aspect in us. And because this feels challenging and uncomfortable, we can react in a defensive or abusive manner, or we instantly want to run or separate from these feelings.

When we feel rejected or hurt by another person in life, it seems easier to blame, judge and separate from someone instead of accepting our part in this experience. The moment we say, 'It's not my problem; it's theirs,' is the moment we give our power away and the opportunity to heal.

When I separate from someone, or when I judge someone because of their point of view, I can miss valuable life lessons and my ability to evolve. And if I continue to ignore the parts of me that have been wounded or rejected, they will be mirrored back to me in my relationships and my experiences in life.

One example of the separation we can have with a family member is 'Hope', who is a client of mine. Hope always felt second-best growing up alongside her brother. Whenever they went out to visit the extended family, her brother was always the centre of attention. No matter what Hope did, her brother always came first. When Hope confronted this injustice with her mother, she was told it was not true or that it was all in her mind.

This left Hope feeling invalidated and constantly unsupported by her mother. It took some time for Hope to understand that the reason her mother did not support her was because she did not have the courage to stand up against the extended family and did not feel strong enough to set boundaries that would protect Hope.

Hope grew up believing that she would not be supported in life nor that her truth would be heard. She grew up seeing that her mother could not stand up against the injustice of life.

This belief led Hope into an abusive relationship, where her husband constantly lied to her. After she finally left this man, taking her three children with her, life continued to mirror this distrust and her inability to stand in her power.

Hope came to see me after her eleven-year-old son had died tragically of cancer. In one of our sessions, I offered to do a soul retrieval to help heal her past wounds and her relationship with her mother. A soul retrieval is simply retrieving a part of us that has become lost or energetically separated after we have faced trauma or tragedy.

This separated aspect occurs when our body shuts down during trauma. The shutdown occurs to protect us and to stop us from facing or feeling what is happening at the time. In doing this, we leave a part of us behind. This separation can present in our adult life as a fear of abandonment, a depression, a distrust in life or a chronic illness.

At times, some of us may have felt there is something missing in life or have felt an emptiness that we cannot fill. And because we do not know how to retrieve this aspect of ourselves, we unconsciously move through life searching for someone or for an experience to fill this void within us.

To retrieve this separated aspect in Hope, I guided her to a memory when she felt unsupported and let down by her mother. It does not matter if the client doesn't remember how old they were at the time or when this separation happened. What matters is the intention and the desire to return this aspect within and feel whole again.

Healing begins each time we acknowledge and nurture the wounded or traumatised child in us. Healing begins each time we allow this part of us to return, knowing that we are worthy to feel whole in life. Of course, we will always remember the trauma, but after healing, we will not hold this trauma in our body memory or continue to attract the stories or experiences that keep us suffering. To complete the healing, I asked Hope to forgive her mother for all the times she did not stand up for her or protect her.

Please note, healing past trauma is a fragile and vulnerable space to work in. Each case is unique, and each client will respond differently. I encourage you to only do this type of healing with trained practitioners in this area.

The next steps towards healing a relationship after a soul retrieval takes patience as we change and develop new behavioural patterns. However, Hope found that after she set new boundaries with her mother a few days after our session, she noticed a positive response in her mother. She noticed there was less tension between them and when Hope needed support the following week, her mother stepped up and told her brother to take care of her. This surprised Hope but also allowed her to trust in life again and in her ability to heal all her relationships.

The truth is while we continue to hope and wait for someone else to change their behaviours, or we continue to fight or demand they give us what we need, we will continue to suffer. Each of us holds the ability to heal and change our relationships in life. We just need to take the time to go within and discover the wounds that keep us trapped.

What I have learned from the First Nations cultures is that they understood long ago we are 'one' with the universe, and everyone and everything in nature is related. However, until we understand that we do not exist as separate entities, we will never feel a deep connection within or with life.

One way we can avoid feeling these rejected or separated parts of ourselves is to create busyness or repetitive behaviours that suppress or distract us from feeling our emotional pain.

I remember when the kids were little, and I was busy with work and life in general, I was often stressed if I did not have time to clean and tidy the house.

So instead of nurturing myself or taking the time to acknowledge my feelings or question why my home needed to be spotless, I ignored this and continued to make it a priority. It took me a long time to recognise that this behavioural pattern was just one way to avoid my fears of not being in control. Cleaning my house gave me a sense of completion and control; however, this was always short lived.

Looking back, if I could give some advice to my younger self, I would say, 'Before you pick up the vacuum or start cleaning, just take a moment to stop, breathe and allow space to acknowledge your feelings. What emotions are coming to the surface? Do you feel that you are not doing enough? Are you doing too much? Do you need to clean? Or do you need to nurture yourself and rest?'

I would have answered yes to all those questions!

It is so important to recognise the patterns we have created to avoid our feelings. We must take note what actions we create next time we feel out of control, stressed or overwhelmed. Is this a habit we have not been aware of? If so, understand how this avoidance is blocking our pathway to wholeness. In the end, we do not need to do more cleaning but rather recognise what is fragmented in us and to seek the right support that will lead us to healing.

In the stillness, I turn the mirror towards me and ask, 'Is this experience or person stirring something in me to learn from? Do I run or separate when life is challenging or confronting?' In this space, I take the time to validate my feelings.

Remember, nothing we are feeling is wrong. Stillness is simply a space to explore, listen and understand ourselves more deeply.

Kahlil Gibran says, 'Life and death are one, even as the river and the sea are one.'[4] Before I started a practice of stillness and listening, I would never have understood this quote; however, it was in the quiet moments of life that I recognised the deep separation I had with life. I saw that I was separated from my authentic self; I saw in my grief, I often felt separated from the flow and the fullness of life and from trusting I would be supported.

When the clouds cover the sun, it may appear there is no sun; however, the sun is always shining. And so, even when we are suffering deeply in life, remember it is our disconnection from the source of life, which is always here, that keeps us in this difficult space. Returning to this source requires us to stop, listen and create room to heal.

When someone shows me their beauty or their laughter, I understand there is beauty and laughter in me. When they show me their fear, pain or anger, I understand there is fear, pain and anger in me.

We were all born in innocence and all share a common longing to be accepted and loved. Each experience we have in life is simply an opportunity to learn and to strengthen our union with everything and everyone.

Questions to ask in Stillness

Remember to find a quiet place to sit with your journal and ask yourself the following questions. You may like to draw or paint any associated feelings that arise:

Who am I separating from and why?
When did this start?
How is this making me feel?
What personality traits does this person have that is also in me?
What feelings am I ignoring or shutting out?
Am I scared to feel this?
What could this experience be teaching me about myself?
How can I heal and return these separated parts of me?
How can I allow myself to feel whole again?

Part Two—Everything is Felt

Moments of Stillness and Movement

When we take the time to be still, peace will move through us like a river.

There is nothing more beautiful than gliding over calm seas on a sailboat. I have only experienced this a few times, but I remember knowing that we were only sailing effortlessly because we were constantly adjusting the sails to flow with life's changes.

Moving with each moment is also like sailing. We need to adapt, adjust and allow the winds of change to move us towards destinations of growth and expansion.

To sail safely, a sailor needs a mixture of specific knowledge, honed skills and a gut instinct to observe the water, wind and weather behaviour.

When the wind is wild and strong, and the sails billow with air, our first response is to control the sails and prevent the boat from tipping; however, a trained sailor's response is to surrender and let go of the sails, which allows the boat to naturally re-balance itself.

And when there is no wind on the water, the sailors call this space 'becalmed'. It is here they learn to be still and patient until the wind rises again. Life too, is made up of these moments and like the sailor, we can either surrender and let go, which re-balances us, or we can resist and try to control life.

However, the world teaches us to live another way and insists we take control and keep moving. In the ebb, it urges us to pull down the sails and jump on to the speed boat. Or in the pauses of life, the world convinces us that life is short and that we will miss valuable opportunities if we do not act immediately. Over time, this forward movement and urgency leads to stress, exhaustion and health issues. It also takes us away from our ability to trust in life and believe it will flow again in the right time.

And when we are not moving frantically to get what we want, the world has conjured up another word and space to live in: 'Waiting'. Waiting keeps us trapped in a future event we believe is better than this moment. How often have we said, 'I'm waiting for…?'

While we continue to believe that this future event will bring us happiness or completion, we will never discover this moment contains everything we need. Just because something is not here right now does not mean it will not arrive later. How interesting that we have a saying: 'I can't wait'. Because the truth is, we can't. It is either here, or it is not.

It is only our minds that convince us something is missing in life, and while we are focused on this, we ignore the wisdom that being present offers. So how do we learn to live in each moment? By moving beneath the surface of our stress and busyness and into stillness, where the fullness of life is always present. In this space of stillness, we remember to slow down and feel, and this allows us to respond to life in a new way. With practice, we can learn to pause before we speak and question our decisions in life, rather than unconsciously reacting and responding from learned behaviours.

Once we recognise the response we are having to a situation, we can take the time to nurture these feelings and shift our perspective. For example, if we are caught in traffic and running late for work, it doesn't matter if we are upset about this. What is important is that we acknowledge the feelings we are having about it. Dropping into stillness before our next action helps us shift our perspective and our thoughts about this situation.

We can do this by taking some deep breaths in and out as we sit in the car, which will slow our thoughts down and allow clarity and patience. From here we can adjust our perspective and remember that this too will pass. When we move with our experiences in life, rather than resist or fight them, we will open our energy field. This will give us space to flow with life again.

Life can either feel full or empty depending on what we are focused on. There will always be desire, wanting and a longing to change our moments of suffering, scarcity or pain. Unfortunately, when we continue to reject unpleasant experiences in life or ignore our feelings about it, we can block energy moving through our body. Over time, this build-up of energy can leave us feeling anxious and stressed.

When we focus on our wellbeing and trust in life, we can connect with the ever-present vibration of fullness. The more we tune into this radio frequency of expansive energy, the more we will shift out of our feelings of emptiness and disconnection. Returning to this source of fullness is something we need to practise again and again.

So, how do we do this? By creating daily practices that help shift and connect us to this energy. Like yoga, which opens our energy, or breathing exercises and meditation. Or being still in spaces like nature. In nature, we can ground our energy and become aware of the stories or fears we are holding on to. In stillness, we have an opportunity to feel, listen and question our suffering. In still moments, we can be moved to understand our next step and the wisdom to achieve this.

Satipatthana (Pali) is a word that is part of the Buddhist practices leading to detachment and liberation and can translate as 'a foundation of mindfulness'. It derives from the root meaning 'to remember'. Pali signifies presence of mind and encourages us to remember to keep the attention inside of us, instead of outside of us.[5] When we practise keeping our attention inside, we learn to strengthen our intuition and do what is right for us. In seeking answers

Moments of Stillness and Movement

outside of us, we can be led down pathways that confuse us and lead us astray.

No matter what we are experiencing in life, when we take the time to 'respond' to our experience rather than 'react' out of fear, or as we learn to 'observe' our feelings rather than engage in the stories that our mind creates about them, we will move through our challenges more easily.

So, how do we know we are present in life? When we become the neutral observer of our experiences and a conscious creator of our decisions. When we are not in this state, we are dragged unconsciously into experiences based on our old beliefs or karmic paths.

Living in each moment doesn't mean we won't feel challenged or wish that life was different. It simply means we allow ourselves to be here, feel it all, and create the time to move into spaces of love and abundance.

Being present, we learn to recognise that life is always moving and evolving, and this is just one small part we are experiencing. Stillness and movement are part of every aspect of life and in nature. They happen in the change of our seasons, floods and famines, births and deaths, droughts and fires. In each season of life, there is no good or bad, only pause and movement.

One place that reminds me of this stillness and movement is by the water. The sea and the river hold beautiful energy, and in this space, I was often guided to receive wisdom that helped me flow with life again.

As the waves rolled towards me, I felt their arms pull me in and call me home. They asked me to surrender, and as the waves moved over me, they guided me out into the unknown.

Out of my comfort zone, and in this infinite space, I felt my fears and limitations arise, but I also felt supported and encouraged to be with it all. I was shown that when the tides change, or I feel like I am drowning, not to struggle or try to control the experience, but to move beneath the surface and into the still dark waters, where wisdom and peace are found.

I understood that the waves on the surface are my experiences in life, but to create balance, I need to move beneath this and allow stillness in as well. The more I learned to trust and heal in these spaces, the more I moved into the deeper waters of understanding.

However, I was also shown that if I was fearful of stepping out of my comfort zone or continued to ignore the call to come home, the sea would swell and the waves crash, leaving me breathless, confused and lost.

Life, like the sea, is unpredictable; yet, when we learn to move deeply with each moment, we will be led into infinite horizons and fullness.

Questions to ask in Stillness

Find a quiet place to sit with your journal and ask yourself the following questions. You may like to draw or paint any associated feelings that arise:

Do I feel uncomfortable when there is no movement in life?
What does stillness teach me about myself?
In the busyness, can I create room to pause, listen and receive what I need?
In the stillness, do I honour and nurture my feelings?
What do I need to let go of?
How can I find room in my life for stillness?
How can I find room in my life for movement?

Moments of Darkness

Wisdom is revealed in the dark, still spaces of life.

In all the cycles of life, it is stillness that teaches me the most about myself.

In these dark, quiet spaces, deep transformation occurs. It is here I discover who I think I am and what is blocking my path towards movement and growth. In this space, I feel my impatience and my limiting stories. It is here that I lean in and acknowledge my fears instead of running from them. It is here I discover where I am separating from the source of my abundance, love and joy.

In the darkness, I plant my seeds of intention, and as they crack open and take root, I open my heart and discover a new direction towards light and growth. Introspection in these dark spaces always reveals what is hidden and allows me to question my direction in life. In this space, I find my resilience and courage. It is here that I learn to adapt and respond to life in a new way.

If I want to expand my future and limit my suffering, I need to be prepared to move into spaces where my vulnerability is felt and my comfort zones of safety are stretched.

Seeds do not germinate in light like they do in darkness because the light decomposes the carbonic acid gas, expels the oxygen and fixes the carbon, which hardens the seed and prevents growth. Some seeds lie in the ground for a whole year before they germinate. However, a seed that does not spend time in the darkness will never evolve.[6] But when we nurture the seed in the right conditions, like the seed of an acorn, it will become a magnificent oak tree.

This is also true for us. When I plant my seeds and ideas in my mind and send them out into the world, often I want an instant response or an overnight success. Yet, without time in still, quiet spaces where nurturing, patience and wisdom develop, I will never strengthen my intuition and my ability to understand the next step.

Like the seeds in the ground, I require certain conditions and processes necessary for growth, a space to witness my thoughts and beliefs and to understand how I respond to life and why I am not receiving what I need. I need a space where I can digest what has been said or has been seen. The darkness is not a place of punishment, but rather a place to find clarity and peace.

Another way to understand growth is to watch a tree lose its bark. For the tree to expand, it must shed its outer layers first. This is a long and patient process, and the bark sheds easily when the tree is ready to expand from the inside out.

Moments of Darkness

Part of my growth is to expand from the inside out as well. And by that, I mean having the courage to make changes in life or doing what is right for me. The more I focus on expanding these authentic aspects of myself, the easier it will be to shed my old ways of being. And even though shedding and letting go can feel vulnerable, as it exposes my inner layers, I have learned to trust in this process and understand this is always my pathway to freedom.

Each time I practise focusing on my potential and the abundance of life, I am less likely to feel overwhelmed when life suddenly changes, or when I feel like I am going backwards. This is just a reflection of the spiral of life.

Everything in life spirals in concentric circles. These spirals are everywhere in nature, from human DNA to the galaxies, from simple to complex substances, and from the microcosm to the macrocosm. A spiral represents the ever-expanding universe and is a symbol of growth and evolution. it is also a symbol of the cycles and rhythms of life.

Each cycle I face in life has a natural order and if I resist the experiences that challenge me or awaken my fears, I block the pathway towards growth. On the days when I feel like I am spiralling, I step back, slow down and allow myself time to understand what is going on in my mind and body.

I acknowledge my feelings and breathe them out. I validate and nurture what feels separated or painful in me. And as I let go, I begin to feel a shift within and move up the spiral again.

Karen Lang

It's important to note that it took years of practice for me to feel comfortable in stillness. After my son died, my busy mind and my overwhelming emotions made it extremely difficult to be still. Fortunately, over time, I felt the calm waters of peace wash over me.

Each of us needs to create small steps towards a stillness practice and be patient as we work out what is enough or what is too much. But the more we practise being here, the more we will flow with life.

The lotus flower is a beautiful symbol of transformation and what can emerge from muddy dark waters. Despite the fears we may have about being in the dark spaces of life, the lotus reminds us it is always possible to rise above our situation and blossom.

Interestingly, the lotus flower signifies 'death' in certain cultures, which again reminds us of the deep changes that healing creates in us. No matter where we are in nature, every river, land, mountain and tree holds expansive energy and ancient wisdom. To receive this, we only need to take the time to be open, still and listen.

Questions to ask in Stillness

Find a quiet place to sit with your journal and ask yourself the following questions. You may like to draw or paint any associated feelings that arise:

What needs to be nurtured in me?
What feelings or painful memories are arising in me?
What feelings need to be shed, forgiven, or released, so I can receive what I need?
Do I need to grow in a new direction?
What am I afraid to feel in the darkness?
Do I need support?
What feels empty in me?
What feels full and beautiful in me?

Moments of Judgement

Judgement has no power over the strength of love and acceptance.

I have always been hard on myself. Looking back, I can see how self-judgement not only affected me but rippled out to everyone around me. The pressure I placed on myself was not from a place of love but from a deep-rooted belief that I was not good enough. And the reason I did not feel good enough was from the belief that I needed to be perfect.

Judgement is the smoke screen that hides rejection and fear. Judgement condemns the rejected parts of us instead of treating ourselves with self-compassion, and the judgement of others is simply a projection of the rejection within us. What we reject in another, we reject in ourselves. As long as our mind is comparing, it will continue to look for weakness in us both.

Judgement is an illusion and an ongoing dialogue in our mind to do better, to be better, and then measure this against perfection. However, when we hold on to these rejected parts in us, we move away from the fullness of life and miss seeing the beautiful light of our own being.

Our fear of rejection stems from the experiences we had growing up. Over time, the unconscious beliefs we made at the time of our experience continue to block us from receiving love and acceptance. Our unconscious judgments can be about money, 'There is never enough'; or work, 'I am responsible for everyone'; or comparison, 'They have more than me'; or looks, 'I will never be attractive enough'.

Low self-esteem is created from a trauma or wound we experienced in childhood. And until we heal this wound and learn to change our self-defeating language and exaggerated narratives, we will continue to stay trapped in our suffering and separation. When we don't value ourselves, when we don't believe we are worthy to receive love and acceptance, the world will mirror this belief back to us and continue the cycle of judgement.

Instead of focusing on what is wrong and separated in us, we need to understand how we can validate and remember what is beautiful and whole in us.

The first step towards healing judgment in myself was to slow down and to recognise the power that these thoughts had over my choices each day. With guidance and support, I found the wounded parts in me that ignited these judgemental behaviours. I found the little girl in me who felt overweight and alone at times. I found the little girl in me who was scared to speak up and share her truth.

Moments of Judgement

It was only when I healed these experiences of rejection in me that I was able to start a daily practice that softened and changed my inner critic and opened my heart to receive.

The first questions to ask are: 'What part of me am I rejecting? Am I rejecting the way I look? The way I work? Who am I judging outside of myself?'

In knowing who or what we are rejecting or judging in our day-to-day life, we will discover what we are rejecting in ourselves. When we limit our capacity to stories of not doing or being enough, we will never explore the unknown potentials in us.

Guilt and shame are also destructive emotions that can separate us from the oneness of life. Indeed, we may internalise such admonishments unconsciously, and this can play out in our relationships as well. And so, it is important to ask ourselves, 'What guilt or shame am I carrying from the past? When did I decide it was my fault that something happened? What do we believe we have to change in ourselves to be loved and accepted?

When we believe we must act, look or behave in a certain way to be accepted, we reject our authentic whole self. Remember our primal brain is designed to protect what feels familiar and comfortable in us. For example, if we say the words, 'I am beautiful', we will never believe this statement on a deep cellular level if we are holding onto childhood or ancestral emotional wounds.

To heal these wounds, we must clear the trauma and the story of rejection in us, and then create a practice to change our judgemental thoughts and behaviour. To do this we can explore soul retrieval therapy, somatic healing, (energy healing) or ancestral healing with a trained practitioner. I speak about this more deeply in the chapter 'Moments of Anxiety'.

Dr Masaru Emoto is a Japanese scientist who revolutionised the idea that our thoughts and intentions impact our physical realm. For over twenty years, Dr Emoto studied the scientific evidence of how the molecular structure in water transformed when it was exposed to human words, thoughts, sounds and intentions.[7]

His work demonstrated how water that was exposed to loving, kind and compassionate human intention resulted in beautiful physical molecular formations in the water. When the water was exposed to fearful, angry and judgemental human intentions, the results were a disconnected, disfigured and unpleasant physical molecular formation.[8]

Dr Emoto's research reveals how the power of human thoughts, sounds and intentions can either strengthen or disempower water molecules, and because the human body is made up of sixty percent water, what we think, judge or believe about ourselves affects every part of our mind, body and spirit.

To create your own research in this area, for a week, write down your thoughts each day and note how many times you judge yourself or another person. Write down how many times you say, 'I can't' or 'This never happens to me' or 'I am not good enough'. You may be surprised

Moments of Judgement

how often you say this to yourself, and how much this impacts who and what you are attracting into your life.

Find the little girl or boy in you that is looking for validation and love outside of yourself. Find the child within who is demanding attention from others. Feel what is wounded or separated in you and speak gently to this child and comfort them.

Creating new behaviours in self-compassion and uplifting mantras can help us focus on the fullness in this moment. We can replace our of old ways of speaking with 'I receive everything I need' or 'I am always enough'. The more we speak from a place of love, truth and abundance, the more we will attract what is rightfully ours.

Judgement is like an old movie that is constantly on replay. And although it seems easier to keep doing this, if we can move through the initial steps and the uncomfortable stages of change, over time we will start to see ourselves through a 'lens' of self-compassion and love.

I never believed I could change my judgemental thoughts, but after ancestral healing and daily meditation, I began to practise speaking differently to myself and love the parts of me that for so long I had ignored.

The following story is a good example of what can happen when we allow judgement to distort the truth.

After holding a big party with friends to celebrate his fortieth birthday, Brian noticed his wallet was missing. At first, he was not concerned and quickly scanned the room. After no success, he went to bed. However, the following morning as he began to search for it more seriously, he began to consider if any of his friends may have taken it by mistake.

His wife Sarah could not think of anyone specifically, but they did consider one friend who had struggled with his finances and a gambling addiction, and wondered if he was in trouble again. Brian began to call some of his friends and suggest that this is what happened. Of course, some agreed that this was possible, and some were not sure. After a day of searching, Brian felt certain that it was his friend with the gambling problem and decided to call him and confront him.

When Brian called his friend to ask how he was going, the friend replied that he was the best he had been in a long time and expressed how proud he felt that he had gone eight months without gambling. At this point, Brian was not listening to his friend or believing him and said, 'Listen, mate, my wallet went missing at our party the other night and we were just wondering if you know anything about it.'

His friend went silent on the other end, which Brian instantly took as a sign of guilt, but after a long pause, his friend replied, 'I am so sorry that you believe it was me who took your wallet, Brian. You and Sarah mean the world to me, and I am so grateful for all the support you have shown me over the years. Even at my lowest point, I never thought of stealing from my friends.'

After hearing his friend's response, Brian went deathly quiet for two reasons: one, because he knew his friend was speaking the truth, and two, because Sarah was standing in

Moments of Judgement

the doorway holding up his wallet and silently mouthing the words, 'I found it!'

No matter what story we believe to be true, it is important to develop a practice of self-enquiry before we action anything. *The Work,* developed by author and teacher Byron Katie, is such a practice. Every time we do *The Work* we become aware of our behavioural patterns and our true nature. *The Work* starts with four simple questions that allow us to examine our judgements and beliefs about ourselves and others:

1. *Is it true?*
2. *Can you absolutely know it's true?*
3. *How do you react; what happens when you believe that thought?*
4. *Who would you be without that thought?*[9]

When we live out the limiting stories and experiences from the past, we can be blinded by the truth in our present situation. Like nature, life is always changing and evolving. Nothing stays the same, and so, when we create thoughts or beliefs that life is always difficult or that we never get what we need, we will begin to expect this as our truth. There are no guarantees in life but there is always an opportunity to shift our perception and be open to learn.

When we take the time to pause and open, we will remember we have all been born from love and that love is always around us. When we feel and acknowledge this truth on a soul level, we will start to break down the walls we have built on fear. We will remember where there are problems, there are also possibilities.

And at the end of our life, we will not be glad we spent our precious time here judging or limiting our infinite potentials. The next time a heavy thought arises, take the time to understand where this wound is hiding within and allow the space to examine these old beliefs.

One way to understand how our beliefs manifest in the world each day is the story of three students. Each student was given a piece of uncarved wood to work with. The first student knew immediately what he was going to create and how it would look, and although he was the first to finish, he spent the rest of his life unsatisfied with the results.

The second student deliberated for months and was overwhelmed by all the choices he had. Each time the student began to create something, he changed his mind. He always believed there was something more to see or something more to feel. In the end, he ran out of wood and of time.

The third student sat in silence with the uncarved wood for a long time. He began to learn about the wood, its history and its natural habitat. Some days he didn't know what to do and some days he did too much. Over time, he understood how to move with the grain and the texture of the wood, rather than moving against it, and realised that doing less was so much more.

At the end of his life, the student finally understood that the goal was not to create a masterpiece with the wood, but rather to see the masterpiece in the uncarved wood.

Moments of Judgement

To discover the divine masterpiece in ourselves, we need time in stillness. We need to recognise how often we use our energy to compare instead of expanding our unique gifts into the world.

From here, we begin to plant seeds of love, and as we patiently water, nurture and wait for these seeds to grow, the weeds of judgment will naturally separate, wither and die.

In this space, we may discover we have only spoken one type of language to ourselves, and in return our heart and soul may reply, 'I want you to feel so much more than the language of rejection.' Do not be afraid to face the rejected parts of self; in doing so, we will reunite ourselves in love and receive love in return.

Questions to ask in Stillness

Find a quiet place to sit with your journal and ask yourself the following questions. You may like to draw or paint any associated feelings that arise:

Where is this wound of rejection in me?
When did it begin?
What do I judge in myself?
What do I judge in others?
What activities create judgement in me?
What activities expand my energy and my thoughts?
How can I stay in this expanded energy of truth of love more often?
Do I need support to achieve this? If so, what is my next step?

Moments of Anxiety

Peace is awakened and nurtured in stillness.

A few years into my grief, I stopped at a red light and felt a wave of anxiety move over me. My heart began to race, my mouth went dry and within a few seconds, I felt panic set in. At the time, I did not know that I was having an anxiety attack, but my first reaction was to run, seek safety and distract myself from those overwhelming feelings.

Even though my son's car accident was a few years earlier, the anxiety moving through me was simply a build-up of my grief, fear and shock, and now this was being expressed in my body.

According to the National Institute of Health, one in three people will experience an anxiety disorder.[10] One reason this anxiety continues to grow in our society is because of our separation between two worlds: our current environment – which is one of busyness, internet addiction and stress – and our connection to healing, nature, tribe and ceremony.

Anxiety is part of our in-built survival instinct. When we are faced with a threatening situation, our brains and body respond to protect us. Our adrenaline starts pumping, our heart starts racing and we enter flight or fight mode. However, if this is occurring daily when there is no danger, then we need to address this and understand why.

When we ignore these feelings, which are our body's way to warn us and signal there is something wrong, at some point like my experience at the stop light, this stored energy will release unexpectedly and overwhelm us.

The sensations of anxiety made me feel like I was going to die, and as my fears heightened, I could feel panic set in. It took me a long time to understand that it was my fear of it, and the resistance to my anxiety, that kept it alive in me.

Claire Bidwell Smith in her book *Anxiety: The missing stage of grief* says, 'Grappling with anxiety is like driving a car on an icy road. When the car begins to skid, you need to turn with it, in order to gain control, rather than trying to veer away.'[11]

In the still moments of meditation, I became painfully aware of my busy mind and my fears. Often, my mind felt like a freight train that would not slow down, and the impulse to move was overwhelming.

When the unease of anxiety takes over, our first reaction is to distract ourselves from our fears and suppress them. We do this by creating busyness, or we suppress our feelings with substances that help shut them out. Either way, this response keeps us trapped in a cycle of suffering.

We need to remember it's okay if we feel stressed or anxious, but we must address the underlying causes of why this is happening.

When we understand that both our heavy and light feelings are just energy, we learn to separate from identifying or attaching a story to the experience we are having. We are not anxious people, we are not angry, stressed or helpless; rather, we are just experiencing the energy of anxiety, anger, stress or heaviness in us.

When we are trapped in fear, we cannot see clearly or see the next step. Anxiety creates panic and uncertainty and keeps us attached to the stories and the illusions of our mind. Often the last thing we feel like doing when we feel overwhelmed or anxious is to slow down and focus on our breath. However, this is exactly what will destroy the power that anxiety has over us.

For me, the road to healing my grief and my anxious energy was a daily practice. It was a space I learned to breathe out my overwhelming feelings and move into the fullness of life. In stillness I would remind myself, 'I am safe,' 'I am supported' and 'I will receive what I need'.

Taking the time to nurture our feelings and anxiety is the first step towards healing. Of course, there will always be 'quick fixes' for our stress and anxiety, but they are simply that, 'quick fixes', and are not long-term healing strategies.

Sometimes we are told that it is 'not normal' to feel overwhelmed, or that we should not feel this much fear or anxiety. But if we continue to ignore or disconnect from these feelings, which are real and are overwhelming to us, it may lead to long-term health issues like PTSD, anxiety disorders or depression.

The truth is, it's more important to address, understand and heal these wounds in us rather than label ourselves and continue to believe there is something wrong with us.

Somatic healing and soul retrieval

One reason we may develop anxiety in life is because of a traumatic experience we had when we were younger. During this experience we may have been separated from one of our parents, abused, or left alone and felt unsafe.

No matter what happened, what is important to understand is how we felt at the time of this experience. If it felt overwhelming, it will be stored in our body's memory. And when we start something new in life, or when separation is involved, it can trigger this fear or stored trauma in our body, which makes us believe we are in this experience again.

Trauma stored in our body's cellular memory is just one way that anxiety can present itself, no matter what age we are.

When we experience trauma or loss, part of our energy can separate from us unconsciously. This happens when the fight-or-flight response is triggered, which is the response our body creates to protect us. However, if we cannot fight against this trauma at the time, then part of us may flee energetically.

Moments of Anxiety

When we do not recognise this separation, we may be confused why we keep attracting in the experiences or people that trigger or mirror this trauma in us. Therefore, it is important to heal the initial trauma so we can have wholesome relationships and abundant experiences.

Over time, somatic healing helps us deepen our connection to body, mind and spirit. Soma is a Greek word meaning 'the living body' and with practice, we can strengthen our body intuition and wisdom. Please note, however, this should only be done or guided by a holistic practitioner trained in this area.

Healing our suffering or anxiety requires time, patience and nurturing. But if we keep suppressing what feels uncomfortable or confronting within, we will never awaken our resilience and strength. We will never recognise the warrior in us, the medicine man or woman in us and our ability to heal.

Dzogchen Ponlop Rinpoche said, 'In the process of uncovering our Buddha nature, we have to be willing to get our hands dirty.'[12]

Life is messy and challenging at times, but when we find the courage to sit with it all and seek the support we need, we will uncover our Buddha nature and find peace.

Questions to ask in Stillness

Find a quiet place to sit with your journal and ask yourself the following questions. You may like to draw or paint any associated feelings that arise:

How much room is anxiety taking up in my life?
What triggers an anxiety attack?
When did this begin?
What actions do I take when I am having anxiety attack?
Am I attached to the story or the identity of anxiety?
Who do I become when I am anxious?
Do I use sentences like, 'I am always anxious?'
If so, how can I let go and begin a new story?
Do I need support to do this?
If so, who would I contact?

Moments of Anxiety

*

In my anxiety, I feel separated from the oneness in life
I feel alone, and fearful
I move away from the situation I am in
I move outside
I sit on the ground; I place my hands on the earth
I say out loud, 'I am here,' 'I am safe'
I feel the strength and support of the earth
I take some deep breaths in and out
My mind is racing, and my body feels out of control
But I remember I have control over my breath
I focus on my breath; I breathe in deeply and out slowly
I ask my spirit guides, angels, and ancestors to be with me
I say again,
I am safe. I am here. I am supported
I remember anxiety is just energy moving through my body
I remember I need to release this energy
I visualise myself in the womb of Mother Earth
Away from all my fears
I remember I am supported, nurtured and safe in this space
I continue to breathe in and out deeply
My heart rate lowers
My body relaxes
I am full again.

Moments of Anxiety in our Children

Resilience awakens in us the moment we step out in courage.

As parents, it is difficult to watch our children suffer with anxiety at any age. Anxiety not only affects how our children feel but how they think about life, and this can create problems at school and home as well as socially.

Anxious children perceive danger at a heightened level, and over time, this can drain both the child and the parents' energy. Anxiety can present as physical symptoms in children such as insomnia, nightmares, diarrhoea, stomach aches and headaches. And because their thoughts and their bodies convince them they are in danger, it is important we approach their healing in a sensitive and creative way.

Karen Lang

Acknowledge and validate their fears

Validating our children's feelings and fears is important because when we dismiss them or say, 'Don't be silly, you will be fine,' they are more likely to shut down their feelings. This can increase their anxiety and create a disconnection from you and their perceived reality.

Children are sensitive to their environment. They are sensitive beings and if there is any stress in the home or problems in the parents' relationships, this can create uncertainty and fear in them. Therefore, instead of saying, 'Mummy I feel unsafe and concerned about you and daddy,' they might say, 'I feel sick and don't want to go to school today.'

As parents, we are responsible for the energy we create in our homes. If we are stressed and overwhelmed, our children will feel it, even when we believe we are hiding it. The greatest results I have found in healing anxiety in children is when the parents take responsibility for healing their own trauma, fear and stress first. It's important to recognise there is no separation between us and our children. Once we understand this, we can take the necessary steps to receive the support we need and help heal our family.

Creating daily practices like stillness, meditation and yoga for ourselves or together with our children can create harmony and balance in our home.

Art Therapy

Creating art is a natural form of communication for most children that can help with a variety of challenging presentations such as personality and emotional disorders, speech and language disorders, childhood trauma, abuse, grief and loss.[13]

Children love creativity, and art is one way they can express their story in a non-confrontational manner. An art therapist can decipher the metaphors and symbolic language that children use to express their environment and themselves, and how their unconscious thoughts and anxieties are presenting to the outside world.

One activity I learned in my art therapy workshops was to ask a child to paint, draw or create a character that is based on how they are feeling. It might be an angry character, a monster, or an anxious, fearful or jealous character. Once the child has created their picture we can ask, 'What is the name of your character?' We can ask them to describe what they have drawn. Ask them, 'What parts do you like about this character?' 'What parts do you not like?' And most importantly, 'What does this character need? Does it need attention or love? How can this character be released and return to its rightful home?'

In asking these questions, we are separating the anxiety from inside the child and creating a space to see their story on the outside. In doing so, the child can share their feelings and their needs in a safe environment, which gives a parent or therapist the opportunity to understand what they need.

As parents, creating art therapy with our children helps us connect and communicate with each other non-verbally. Sitting together creates quality time, and when they feel nurtured, children are much more likely to open us and trust they will be supported.

Nature therapy for children

If our children do not like spending time nature, it usually stems from an experience they have had in the past, or from not growing up having experiences in nature. Nature is a creative playground for all our needs, and when we create fun activities for our children in nature, they learn to feel safe to express their feelings and find creative ways to heal.

Nature therapy is healing for both adults and children and is essentially art therapy outdoors. In nature, we can teach our children about stillness, mindfulness and the signals that life shows us. We can use examples of a caterpillar, butterfly, spider or plant to teach them about transformation, life cycles and the impermanence of life. In nature we can teach them to express their individuality and their unique language, like each of the insects or animals do naturally. We can teach them how the trees and the plants adapt to and rejuvenate in difficult situations and environments.

By creating art in nature, our emotions can be externalised, and this allows us to process our feelings more easily and find creative resolutions.

Ancestral Healing

If the family home and parents are doing well, and the anxiety in our children appears to have no known cause or reason, or nothing helps heal this, it may be a good time to explore ancestral healing. Often an ancestral trauma will appear in only one child in our family; however, this may not have been seen in our family history before. Therefore, it may be difficult to understand why this has happened.

Trauma can be transmitted across generations. In other words, what one generation does not heal is likely to be passed on to the next generation. Research indicates that PTSD runs in families, and children of trauma survivors with PTSD are more likely to develop PTSD.

Seek trained practitioners who understand this area of healing and can guide you to release ancestral wounds and step forward into freedom. I write more about this in the chapter 'Ancestral Healing'.

Moments in Nature

Being in nature is simply the greatest space
to heal and expand.

Growing up in South Australia, my home was next to a busy main road, and apart from playing in our backyard, I did not spend much time in nature. However, in the summer, our family spent a lot of time at the beach, and to this day, I have a deep connection to the ocean and its healing power.

It was not until after my son's death that I felt drawn to spend time in nature again, away from my grief and the busyness of my mind.

It took me a long time to trust that when I sat in stillness either in bushland, by the sea or in the park, this would help calm my busy mind and create room to heal my grief and separation from life. When I was alone in the stillness of nature, my feelings and thoughts were heightened, which often made me feel uncomfortable and anxious.

However, the more I practised sitting in these quiet spaces, where everything is felt deeply, the more peace and clarity I felt afterwards.

If I felt anxious in this stillness, instead of leaving and going home, I learned to focus on my breath and breathe out this energy. Each time I took the time to move and breathe through my difficult feelings or thoughts, I started to feel a resilience and strength grow within me.

I discovered that sitting on the grass in the backyard or in the manmade park down the road felt different from being in natural bushland, the ocean, the river or in a forest. In these spaces, I felt expanded and energised. I found it calmed my energy more quickly and when I left, my mind felt clear and open. Over time, this allowed me to find a deeper understanding of myself and life.

Being in nature also helped me see the false identities I played out for others. I saw my vulnerability and my need to be accepted. I also saw how mother nature is always evolving, and this helped me trust that I could evolve and heal too.

Sitting in nature showed me what I needed to let go of and gave me the wisdom to know how. Being there, I began to see what was light and beautiful in me. Out in nature, my heart opened, and I began to feel at home within myself and one with life.

In the stillness, no matter if I was by a river, near a tree, in bushland or at home, I learned to acknowledge that everything I felt was important, whereas in the past, I ignored my fears and feelings because I did not know how to face them or heal them.

As I allowed my relationship with Mother Nature to grow and strengthen, I saw how this was also healing my relationships with others. I understood that as I peeled back the layers and saw my authentic self, I saw this in others as well. I began to feel my life flow more easily like the river I was near. In nature, Mother Earth births out the old in us and moves us into the fullness within and around us.

Growing up, most of us were not taught about the healing benefits that nature can have on our mind, body and spirit. We may have been taught that being in nature was not safe or that it is uncomfortable and dirty. No matter what beliefs we have held onto, discover for yourself the unseen vibration and energy in nature, which holds ancient wisdom and healing. And the more we are in this energy, the more we will flow with life.

Mother Nature provides our food, our water and our ability to breathe. She gives us room to relax and increases our vitality, and because of this, our only response should be to deeply respect and nurture this land we live on.

In our quest to be accepted in society and to live up to the world's standards of success, we have slowly weaned ourselves away from nature and from our ability to nurture the land and ourselves. Perhaps unconsciously, we still believe that being in nature is associated with childish behaviour or wasting time and energy. At some point, we were told to grow up, get a job and become successful, which over time normalised our separation from Mother Nature, our source of life on this planet.

Deep understanding can be found in all our relationships with life; however, once we have lost our connection to this, we can easily live out our limiting karmic stories, and trauma. Often it takes a tragedy or illness to remind us to slow down and evaluate what is important in life.

Transformation and change are patient work, and so, it is important to take small steps. Finding time to practise 'being' and sitting in nature seems difficult at first, and with work commitments, family and the busyness of life, there will always be a reason why we cannot find time to be in this life-giving space.

Often all it takes to create room for this is to question what we do each day. When I am with a new client, they are always surprised how much energy and time they are giving to their old beliefs and behavioural patterns. But when they are willing to let go of their pressure to please others and to let go of the responsibilities and obligations they carry for others, time expands.

Once they begin a regular practice, and see the immense benefits it is having on their physical and mental health, they always feel motivated to do this more often.

It's important to be gentle on ourselves in the beginning of any practice as we remember it takes repetition and patience to create new neural pathways in our brain, and the discipline to keep going.

I started sitting with bare feet on the grass. I practised short, mindful walking meditations in nature before or after work. I sat and placed my hands on the earth. I closed my eyes and felt the stillness of the earth arise in me.

I used breathing exercises as a tool to relax my nervous system and release heavy energy. The changes in me were slow and subtle, but over time, they became motivational and powerful. Each day in nature, as in life, is different, but each moment we are present to holds infinite possibilities and healings.

Grounding in Nature

Scientific research has revealed that 'earthing' or 'grounding' has a positive effect on our health.

Modern lifestyle practices such as shoes, stress and busyness separate us from the powerful vibration of Mother Earth. Studies have shown that this disconnect may be a major contributor to physiological dysfunction and physical problems. When we connect to the earth's electrons, it creates a feeling of wellbeing and a feeling of coming home within. From walking barefoot on the grass to sitting in nature, these simple practices all have the potential to heal us.[14]

Clint Ober, who has studied the science of grounding over many years says, 'When we are grounded, the first result is that it calms our sympathetic nervous system. With practice, this allows our adrenals to recover, which lowers inflammation and pain in our body. However, when our adrenals are exhausted from stress and anxiety, there is too much stimulation in the body and our sympathetic nervous system goes into overdrive. From here, we end up with fatigue, and this is the precursor to all disease in our body, including weight gain.'[15]

Grounding has helped me in many ways. It calms my nervous system, increases my energy each day, clears my mind and helps me sleep more soundly.

Questions to ask in Stillness

Remember to find a quiet place to sit with your journal and ask yourself the following questions. You may like to draw or paint any associated feelings that arise:

How often do you take the time to sit still in nature?
What are you afraid to feel in the stillness?
Can you find compassion, patience and understanding for these feelings?
When do you create time for yourself and to nurture your needs?
Can you think of some spaces in nature where you feel connected and peaceful?

Ancestral Healing

*To create a new future, we must be willing to face
and heal our past.*

My younger sister has always been interested in our ancestry and where we have come from and who we have become because of this. In her research to understand this more deeply, she discovered there was a long history of unexpressed and unhealed grief in our family. This was important information to find as it helped us understand how grief had continued to manifest in each generation. From here we began to investigate how we could heal the trauma of the past and prevent this from happening in future generations.

No matter who we are, our ancestral past carries a strong imprint within our DNA. This can manifest in our life as emotional, physical or spiritual imprints, but when we understand where these wounds or emotional trauma came from, it can reveal a deeper understanding of who we are and our purpose here on earth. It can also help us to access our potential to step into a better future.

When we learned that ancestral healing offered a powerful opportunity to let go of the old beliefs and trauma that our family was carrying, it became an opportunity to expand the intergenerational wisdom and healing gifts we were carrying. We learned that when we healed the wounds and trauma from our blood ancestors who once lived here on earth, we could change the patterns of our past and awaken new behavioural patterns in our future.

Consciously or unconsciously, we are all paying the debts of our past. And while we continue to carry the burdens and invisible cords of our 'unhealthy ancestors', who are ancestors that died from suffering, disease, broken hearts and abuse growing up, we will continue to repeat their injustices, tragedies, diseases and suffering. The 'evolved or healthy ancestors' are the ancestors who lived a happy and healthy life and died in the same way. These 'evolved' ancestors were alive before times of war and were not fearful of who they were and what they were capable of.

These evolved ancestors can become light beings and guides in our spiritual practice, and they can help us awaken what is abundant, healthy and happy in us.

Like the seeds in nature that carry life from one generation to another, so are the voices and traumas of my ancestors carried forward through generations. Each time someone is born into my lineage, they inherit an imprint of the past and a responsibility to change the future.

Aside from the obvious traits like my physical appearance and psychological tendencies, I have also inherited 'familiar life patterns' from my ancestors. These might be positive traits like optimism and abundance or more painful influences like disease or scarcity.

As my sister and I learned how to heal and release these inherited ancestral wounds, one of the areas we worked on was the wound of skin cancers in our family DNA. My grandmother on my father's side, who had an English complexion, was prone to skin cancers. This genetic imprint was passed on to my father and to me as well.

Later in life, my grandmother had a skin cancer emerge on her arm, but for some reason she allowed this to grow without treatment. When she finally did have it surgically removed, she was in a nursing home, and a few days after surgery, the wound became infected and developed into septicaemia, taking her life.

The first skin cancer I had cut out of my body was shortly after our son died in 2001, which looking back makes sense, as the trauma and stress of my son's death awakened this gene in my DNA. And from that day onwards I continued to have several skin cancers a year cut out of my body.

This is just one example of many that can be carried in our lineage, and yet, we often believe this is something we should accept. Instead, my sister and I questioned it. We asked, 'Why did our grandmother let this skin cancer grow?' 'Why did she not take care of this skin cancer and nurture her body?' These generational behaviours and beliefs she held onto and died with explain why it continued to be passed down to future generations.

In our research and daily energy healing practices, we understood that to release this gene within our DNA we had to release the story and belief we were carrying for our grandmother. One of the beliefs my grandmother held was that she was not worthy to nurture herself. She lost her brother when she was quite young. And because of the strict beliefs about not showing your emotions in that generation, she held onto a lot of guilt and unexpressed grief for her brother.

To heal this in our family lineage, my sister and I sat together, lit a candle on our altar and asked our 'evolved healthy ancestors' to be with us and allow this healing in our family.

We asked them to take the wounded story out of our DNA, and then we forgave our grandmother for holding this suffering and asked the healthy ancestors to help heal her in the afterlife. In doing this, we believe we energetically lifted an imprint and belief off our DNA. Of course, we didn't know if we healed this in ourselves so we had to measure this against our reality.

At my next check-up at the dermatologist several months after this healing, for the first time in ten years, I did not have a skin cancer to cut out. I continued to monitor this healing, and the following year, I had another check up with the same results. There we no skin cancers on my body to cut out.

Ancestral Healing

This is just one of the many healings my sister and I have experienced since we have been doing ancestral energetic healings.

Please note, these healings and findings we have discovered are not from any 'one' source, but from various teachings and the wisdom of elders. The good news is that this information is now being discovered both in the science and spiritual sectors. My sister and I are both energy healers who have worked with clients for many years; however, I do not encourage anyone to do this type of healing alone. I encourage you to only do this with trained practitioners in this area.

Another example of how ancestral healing can cure the physical body is shown in 'Anna', one of my clients.

Fourteen months ago, Anna was admitted into the Emergency Room with heart palpitations that were making her cough. After tests were performed and she was examined by the doctors, it was determined that Anna had an ectopic heartbeat. An ectopic heartbeat is where there are changes in a heartbeat that is otherwise normal. These changes can lead to extra or skipped heartbeats. At present, there is often no clear cause of this or a solution for these changes.

They told Anna that if it continued, she should follow it up with her GP.

After experiencing this problem for several months, Anna decided to see her local doctor, who diagnosed this as a 'standard ectopic heartbeat'. However, although Anna found this extremely uncomfortable, the doctor said there was nothing she could do.

Tragically, a few months later, Anna's eleven-year-old daughter passed away suddenly. And while she tried to cope with her overwhelming feelings of grief and loss, her ectopic heartbeat went on in the background, keeping her up at night and uncomfortable during the day.

Ten months later with no relief from this ectopic heartbeat, Anna came to see me to learn how to cope with her grief and to have energy healing. During our first session, I felt an energetic hook on the back of Anna's heart, and as I explained this to Anna, she shared with me about the physical issue she had with her heart. Often these energetic cords I can feel on people's back are an ancestral wound or trauma from the past. Of course, we carry this energetic wound unconsciously, and instead, it may present as a physical problem or a mental health issue.

We called in Anna's 'healthy ancestors' to help heal this trauma in her DNA and we forgave the 'unhealthy ancestors' who carried this. Instantly Anna felt this energy lift off her back and since this healing, she has not had an irregular heartbeat. But I do not encourage anyone do this type of healing, unless they are with an experienced ancestral healer.

To understand ancestral healing more deeply, we can be grateful for two scientists, Mosh Szyf and Michael Meaney, who in 1992 considered a hypothesis as improbable as it was profound. They asked, 'If diet and chemicals can cause epigenetic changes in humans, then why can't certain behavioural experiences as well?'[16]

They considered, 'Could child neglect, drug abuse or other severe stresses, like PTSD, also set off epigenetic changes to the DNA inside the neurons of a person's brain?' These questions turned out to be the basis of a new field in science called, 'behavioural epigenetics'.[17]

According to the new insights of behavioural epigenetics, traumatic experiences in our past, or in our recent ancestors' past, leave molecular scars adhering to our DNA. The mechanisms of behavioural epigenetics underlie not only deficits and weaknesses but strengths and resiliencies, too.[18]

The molecular scars that carry disease or scarcity from our ancestors do not heal or lessen over time but rather continue to move through each generation. And because these behavioural patterns are often lived out unconsciously, they continue to pass on unseen. It is not until we become aware of this, or that this is no longer our burden to carry, that we have an opportunity to release it.

Doing this work, I have found that our sadness and suffering are not necessarily a by-product of the story we are now living but rather the story we are carrying from the past.

So how do we heal our ancestral wounds? When we feel we no longer want to carry the burdens or behavioural patterns of our blood ancestors, we will know it is time to seek ancestral healing. Ancestral healing is done through ritual, ceremony, forgiveness and prayer.

Karen Lang

In my daily practice, I honour and forgive those who have walked before me and see the deep wounds they carried. I understand I have the power to release anger, unworthiness, grief or sickness from the past. I also understand I have the power to expand my healthy DNA that carry my abundance, health and joy, which allows me and my children to step into our potential. Each time I honour and heal my past, I open and embody the gifts of my healthy ancestors.

Another way I have learned to honour my ancestors is by creating an altar in my home. An altar can be a simple and a beautiful expression of how we honour those who have gone before us. At its most essential, an altar is simply a raised structure that serves as a resting place for meaningful objects. My altar is a small box with a cloth over it. It holds the four elements of matter: fire, a candle; air, a feather; earth, bark or dirt from the earth; and water, a bowl of water.

Each element represents the four directions in life. The east, west, north and south. On my altar, I place pictures of those who have passed, and I also lay crystals and rocks that hold energy. My altar is a meeting place where I honour all life. It is a place I set intentions, and a place where ceremony expresses my gratefulness to spirit and to all those who have gone before me and will go after me.

At times I offer food, flowers, tobacco, herbs or essences on the altar as gifts of gratitude. This is a wonderful way to connect with my heritage and culture. Another

Ancestral Healing

form of ancestral healing is understanding and honouring the ancestors of the land I am living on.

Cultural practice acknowledges traditional custodianship of the land at the commencement of functions, meetings and presentations of government departments and various organisations. This acknowledgement pays respect to the traditional custodians, ancestors and continuing cultural, spiritual and religious practices.

Whatever path we take towards healing, each of us has an opportunity to release and heal the threads that link us to paths that no longer serve us. When we take responsibility for this, we not only create healing for ourselves, but for our family's future generations.

And so, we can ask, 'What behavioural patterns have been in my family for too long? Do I want to carry this burden in me any longer? Am I ready to heal this in myself and for my children's children?

A simple enquiry is all it takes to change our life.

Questions to ask in Stillness

Find a quiet place to sit with your journal and ask yourself the following questions. You may like to draw or paint any associated feelings that arise:

What ancestral wounding or behavioural patterns am I carrying?
Do I need to carry these burdens anymore?
What changes do I need to make to heal these wounds from the past?
Do I need support or guidance to help heal these ancestral wounds?
What future do I want for myself and my children?
Am I ready to step into my deepest abundance and potential?

Ancestral Healing

*

When the winds whisper your name
Or you feel the pull of your soul to move in a certain way
Be still and listen.
The echoes of your ancestors are calling you
They summon you to hear the truth.
And to change the stories
Long ago given, but not forgotten,
Let their wisdom move you out of illusion,
And into the heartbeat of your deepest potential.

Moments of Truth

For the river to reflect the beauty of the sky, it must be still;
so too, must we be still, to reflect the universe inside of us.

When Nathan died, my family and I were never prepared for the overwhelming feelings of grief, and we had no idea how to heal. In fact, I think most people would admit they are not prepared for the suffering we face in life, or the grief that comes after death.

While there are many factors at play as to why we suffer, perhaps the most important factor I have learned through healing is that suffering stems from a fear of facing our emotions and learning to be with them.

No matter who we are or what circumstances we face, we will all encounter suffering. Even the first noble truth of Buddhism says that suffering is inevitable; however, even though this is true, how long we suffer is a choice. The Four Noble Truths are a contingency plan for dealing with the physical, mental and emotional suffering that humanity faces.

In Buddhism, it said that desire and ignorance are the root of all suffering. By desire, Buddhists refer to the way we crave pleasure, material goods and immortality, all of which can never satisfy us. Ignorance, in comparison, relates to not seeing the world as it is, but more importantly, ignorance is not taking responsibility for how we think, act and speak in the world.[19]

Some of the ways we suffer are by holding on to thoughts that keep our vibration and our energy low, like feelings of guilt, fear, anger or resentment. Everything that creates suffering begins with a thought, and these thoughts can keep us spinning into a downward spiral. Our thoughts then move into our body as a vibration, which over time, becomes a belief. If we continue to hold on to this belief, it may manifest chronic physical symptoms or mental health issues that over time keep us stuck in our pain.

Our thoughts and expectations of life are the vibrations that we feed out into the world. Even though we may do this unconsciously, we in turn attract likeminded vibrations into the experiences we are having. We cannot have one without the other. It is the law of attraction.

For example, when we hold on to guilt, we are self-loathing, self-criticising and constantly punishing ourselves. This lowers our energy vibration and attracts people or situations that confirm and mirror this belief back to us.

To raise our vibration and alleviate our suffering, I discovered that the first step is to slow down and question why we are suffering. What thoughts and beliefs are we feeding out into the world? What are we receiving back?

And what changes or practices do we need to do each day to become aware of our thoughts and actions and change them to higher vibrations of love and peace?

Many of us search the world to find relief from our suffering. Unfortunately, no matter where we go or who we go to see, our emotions and wounds will still be our responsibility to face and heal day by day.

I experienced a huge shift in my suffering when I understood that I was responsible for healing it. And although I knew that the death of my son was not my fault, it was a daily practice of stillness and meditation that allowed me to discover I had control over my thoughts, my beliefs and my actions. Each time I created changes in myself and found new ways of seeing life, I learned to separate my illusions and blame from the truth. I learned I was resilient and strong.

It would have been easy to stay trapped in my story of suffering if I hadn't understood that I had the power to change my old thought patterns and awaken my authentic self. It took time and patience for me to see I was not a powerless victim, but rather a student of life who needed to become aware of the warrior within me.

Each time I discovered a new layer of my authentic truth, I began to make healthier choices in life, and this helped attract in more love and abundance.

Growing up, we were all given a limited version of our potential, but often this is the one we accept and believe is the truth. The fact is we are so much more than what we have been taught. We have so much more to discover about ourselves than the story we have been given. The only way we will discover our true essence and power is to question why we do the things we do each day. Or why we make the choices that lead us into suffering and rejection.

A short story to understand this potential in us is about an eaglet who fell out of his nest one day and was left orphaned and abandoned in the forest. Shortly after, a large python found the eaglet and decided to take care of him.

As the eaglet grew, the snake knew of the eagle's great power and his ability to soar to great heights. However, the snake kept this knowledge hidden from the eaglet and instead seduced him with another story. Each day the snake taunted the eaglet and only shared stories about his own power and his ability to seduce and kill. Over time, the eaglet grew weak and fearful of the snake and his presence.

As the eaglet absorbed and believed the stories told by the snake, he slowly lost his ability to listen to his intuition and the power to soar freely in the sky, and by the time he became an eagle, he had forgotten who he was.

However, one night as the eagle slept, a great ancestor 'Kunji' came to him in a dream. Kunji took the young eagle to the top of the highest mountain and showed him how the sky unfolded into a limitless horizon. He looked deeply into the young eyes of the eagle, and said, 'Why are you living out the limiting stories you have been told when you are a majestic beast who lives and reigns in the expansive abundance of the sky?'

The young eagle told Kunji that he feared the snake and its ability to kill him. The ancestor laughed and said, 'How can an eagle be afraid of a snake? My son, great power lives within your DNA. You hold the strength and the wisdom of all those who have gone before you. Do not disrespect or ignore the sacrifices your ancestors have made for you or the gifts they have passed on to you. This deep wisdom and understanding will awaken in you every time you step out in courage and fly wing to wing with the great spirit.

'Tomorrow, you will pick up the snake with your talons and take him high upon the mountain and release him. In this space, where your true potential lives, the snake will have no power over you.'

The following morning, the eagle felt empowered and ready to change his destiny. As he approached the snake, it hissed loudly at him and immediately sensed this new power in the eagle, but before he could seduce him, the eagle picked up the snake and released him from the top of the mountain.

When the eagle let go of the snake, something awakened in him, and as his wings expanded, he flew towards the light of the rising sun and remembered who he was.

Our limitations in life are lifted the moment we step out in courage. In doing so, our ability to soar is expanded in us and we can remember who we are. In stillness, we will discover that our mind is full of constant chatter and thoughts about the past, present or future.

Our subconscious mind is responsible for ninety-five percent of our daily habits, thoughts and fears. To awaken these unconscious behaviours, we need time to see the patterns in ourselves and the stories we have held onto as our truth. The first time we enter stillness is the most difficult because our minds are busy and will insist we move back to the familiar safety of our comfortable patterns.

Often our thoughts and fears become louder in these still spaces. Because of this, most people never go beyond the first stage, simply because they do not see immediate changes or results. Developing new pathways in our brain requires patience, consistency and discipline. Do we look like a body builder after two weeks at the gym? No, we do not. And so, we need to practice daily so that our mind, body and spirit feel comfortable in a new way of being.

One way to support a meditation practice is by interrupting thought patterns. For example, when my mind is busy, I interrupt my thought patterns in my meditation by saying the word 'Breathe' out loud each time I breathe in. I repeat this until I am focused on my breathing and my mind becomes comfortable in the stillness once more.

For us to become the observer in life, the one who sees the stories and the behaviours we want to change, we need to slow down enough to understand what they are so we are not a slave to our old ways. And we must remember to not be so hard on ourselves. We all have busy minds, and our only job is to remember to practice!

Stillness is where we will find clarity and an opportunity to connect to the universal vibrations of love, truth, peace and abundance.

Feelings that keep our vibration low
Fear
Anger
Resentment
Guilt
Separation
Anxiety and stress

Actions that keep our vibration high
A focused and disciplined practice
Stillness in nature
Grounding
Yoga
Prayer
Chanting/Mantras/Breathing
Meditation
Life Coach

Questions to ask in Stillness

Find a quiet place to sit with your journal and ask yourself the following questions. You may like to draw or paint any associated feelings that arise:

Am I ready to let go of the limiting stories that keep me suffering?
What stories do I tell myself and what thoughts do I have each day?
How do these stories make me feel when I believe them?
What type of people or situations am I attracting when I feel like this?
What disciplines or practices could I begin to raise my vibration?
When will I start?
Will I require support to stay on this higher vibration? If so, who will I do that with?

Part Three—Everything is Seen

Our Hidden Treasure

What is hidden in me, is hidden in you.
What is found in me, is found in you.

When I was a young mum, I felt insecure about not doing or being enough, and if someone asked me how I was, I sometimes felt I had to tell them how busy I was. Of course, my friends did not put this pressure on me, I did, and I was the only one who needed to change this.

How often have we hidden an aspect of ourselves or lied about something to someone else simply because we did not want to expose our vulnerabilities or share our conflict with another?

When we hide our authentic truth, we will never find our authentic treasure, nor will we discover this authenticity in others. When we reveal to one another our fears and vulnerabilities, we feel a deep sense of connection within.

In this space of truth, our time together becomes sacred and our hearts open. When we do this, we feel comfortable and free to express our unique perspectives in life.

Of course, it is never easy to be vulnerable with another, and often we feel pressured to stick to the story everyone knows and the one we feel most comfortable with. Unfortunately, over time, this creates conflict within us and can present as a physical ailment or mental anguish.

To change this in myself, I started to observe the conversations I had with others and noted where I felt I had to say more, or where I felt shut down by another. I noticed how uncomfortable I felt around conflict and how quickly I conformed to placate a situation.

After Nathan's death, I no longer had the energy to live out the false pretences I had placed on myself. It took many years for me to understand why I was afraid of conflict and of being authentic, but this became the pathway to my freedom.

In silent moments I would ask, 'What stories have I grown up believing about myself? Why am I afraid to reveal my deepest fears and thoughts with others? Am I being pressured by others to be a certain way, or am I placing this pressure on myself? How can I let down my protective walls and speak my truth?'

It wasn't easy at first. For so long I did not have the courage to speak up and I certainly didn't believe I would be heard. But each time I pushed past my fears, I discovered it wasn't as hard as I imagined. If anything, I found these fears and thoughts were universal and left me questioning, 'Why are we all pretending?'

Our Hidden Treasure

Each time I let down my guard and spoke my truth, I realised I felt less judged and rejected. Over time this allowed my confidence to grow. The more I practised being authentic, the more I noticed others felt comfortable to be open and vulnerable too. I began to see not only the treasure I offered the world, but the treasure that others offered me.

One example of finding this treasure is a story about the spiritual shamans who passed on messages to the people from the gods of the mountain. The gods told the shamans that they had created a treasure and that this would be available for everyone to receive. They also said that those who were committed to finding this treasure would discover the secret to life.

However, the people were told this treasure would not be easy to find. The treacherous journey that the gods created to find this treasure could only be completed by those who had immense courage, strength and patience.

Those who truly knew the meaning of this potential within them would also share this treasure for the benefit of everyone they met. And so, the gods hid the treasure in a small cave in the mountain and waited to see who would find it.

When the people in the village heard about this treasure, an excitement moved through the entire community and had everyone wondering who would discover it. One group of men, in their haste to be first, went up the mountain unprepared. In doing so, some men died along the way, and some returned sick and weak and never recovered.

Some went to bed at night, dreaming of the finding this treasure and felt excited about the power they would have over everyone. But by the morning their fears of failure, and their fears of being vulnerable and of death, were too overwhelming.

However, there was one man who decided to approach this differently. He began his journey at the foot of the mountain where he honoured the gods who created this abundance. He made daily offerings and chanted prayers of gratitude for their generosity. Each day he asked to be guided and protected along his journey and listened and waited for any signs that were offered.

This pleased the gods of the mountain, and they sent signals and messages to the man to begin his journey. The next day, as the man began his trek up the steep mountain and towards the treasure, a group of people in the village began to taunt him and told him he that he would never make it. But the man ignored their words and trusted in his intuition.

Along his journey, there were many days where he felt too weak to go on. There were cold and lonely nights where he feared for his life and did not believe he had the courage to go on.

However, each time he surrendered and faced his fears of death and of failing, he felt courage and strength rise in him. And when he felt broken and overwhelmed, he asked for help, and each time he received this, he began to trust he would be supported.

During the final night on the mountain, he dreamed the exact location of the treasure. The next morning, as he entered the cave, he found a rare and precious stone.

But it was not until he came down from the mountain and took the time to contemplate his long and treacherous journey that he recognised the real treasure he had found: the expansion of his wisdom, courage, strength, authenticity and infinite potential. And from that day on, he not only shared the abundance he received from the precious stone he'd discovered but shared his gifts of authenticity and wisdom with all those he met.

Stepping out into the unknown or speaking our truth to others takes courage, but before we find this courage, we need to understand what it is that is holding us back from speaking our truth. What is it we are hiding, not only from ourselves, but also from others?

Becoming aware of the stories and behaviours that we learned growing up is important if we want to create change and awaken our authentic nature. And please remember that undoing what we have always done takes time and practice.

Finding our treasure – our authenticity – although difficult at times, is the greatest gift we can give each other.

Karen Lang

Questions to ask in stillness

Find a quiet place to sit with your journal and ask yourself the following questions. You may like to draw or paint any associated feelings that arise:

What old beliefs or stories do I still believe about myself?
How do I feel when I speak my truth?
How do people react when I am vulnerable with them?
What treasures lay hidden in me that are not seen by myself or others?
Do I have the courage to step out into the unknown and find this treasure?
Do I trust I will be guided? If not, why?

Responsibility

To step into our responsibility, we must first step out of the old stories we are carrying about our responsibility.

As I began to heal from my grief and gain a deeper understanding of life and myself, I started to believe I 'should' help others who were suffering with grief. I felt passionate about sharing the wisdom I had learned and began to give talks at grief seminars. I also led art therapy classes for parents who were grieving.

After these events, I often felt frustrated because everyone was at a different stage in their grief, and it was difficult to help everyone. Although, when I took the time to step back and question my motives, I realised I was trying to fix people. I believed it was my responsibility to teach them how to heal. Instead, I learned that everyone has a unique journey through their grief and no matter how much support we give another, they still need to do the work themselves.

A beautiful example of moving through this transformation alone is a story of a man who found a cocoon and decided to watch and wait for the butterfly to emerge. The next morning a small opening appeared, and the man sat and waited for several hours as the butterfly struggled to force its body through the little hole of the cocoon. It was difficult to watch. Then suddenly, the butterfly stopped moving.

It appeared that the butterfly had pushed as far as it could, and so, the man decided to help it along. He took a pair of scissors and snipped off the remaining bit of the cocoon, allowing the butterfly to emerge easily. But upon closer attention, he saw that it had a swollen body and small shrivelled wings.

The man continued to watch the butterfly because he expected at some point, that the wings would enlarge and its body would return to normal size. Sadly, neither happened, and the butterfly spent the rest of its life crawling around with a swollen body and shrivelled wings, never to fly.

In his kindness and haste, what the man did not understand was that the restriction of the cocoon and the struggle the butterfly went through as it squeezed through the small opening was exactly what it needed to force the fluids from its body, thus allowing its wings to expand and fly.

When we believe we are responsible for other people's pain or suffering, and make this our life purpose, we lose sight of the bigger picture. We don't see that while we are busy trying to fix others, we take away their ability to discover their resilience and purpose in life. We don't see that

Responsibility

while we are running around and looking after others, we stop nurturing ourselves and listening to our own needs and wisdom.

Of course, we can support and guide others through their suffering, but when we continually intervene and try to make it easier for them, we stop transformation in both of us and our potential to fly.

The truth is when we do not set boundaries in life or take responsibility for our own needs, we can be left feeling depleted, resentful and unsupported.

It's always uncomfortable watching someone we love suffer. But if we keep rescuing them every time they are in trouble, over time, they will lose confidence in themselves and their ability to move through transformation and discover their wings.

One example of taking on too much responsibility is a story about a woman who was always taking care of someone or something. She was a widow with two grown children. She had a son, twenty, who still lived at home, and a daughter, thirty, who was married with two children.

And although she loved helping everyone, on the days she felt overwhelmed by all the work this involved, she unconsciously started to pass on this responsibility to her son. Over time, the son began to feel burdened and resentful towards his mother and of the responsibility she gave him, without asking.

One day the son asked his mother what she would do when he left home. He shared his concern that while she helped everyone around her, she in turn ignored her own needs. He said how much this worried him and that he believed this would eventually catch up with her.

This conversation opened a deep wound of fear in the mother, and she asked, 'Who am I if I am not responsible for everyone? What do I do with my time if I am not looking after everyone else?'

This story will seem familiar to many of us because all of us were given a role to play when we were growing up. Some of us took on the responsibility for everyone else, and some of us learned to sit back and let others do all the work.

Of course, the opposite to this story is not taking any responsibility for our choices in life, and this may manifest as everything being someone else's fault. Or that failure is never the result of the choices we have made but rather because of someone else. Over time, this belief leads to low self-esteem, a victim mentality and an ongoing pressure on our family or friends to do everything for us.

Patience and compassion are essential as we begin to understand who we are in life and recognise the beliefs we have been given in childhood. An analogy of this was seen in my backyard one day. As I was sitting outside in my backyard, I watched a crow fly back and forth over my head. After a few minutes, I realised it was building a nest for its family. A crow's nest is built in an astounding array of places, from the eaves of skyscrapers to the crooks of well-concealed tree limbs.

The crow pulled twigs from a tree behind me and then carried the twigs in his mouth to the nest in another tree. I was amazed at its focus and how nothing distracted the crow from its mission of preparing a strong foundation for the future.

It reminded me how patient and focused I needed to be as I let go of my old beliefs that did not support me in life and learned to re-build strong, new foundations based on my truth and authentic self.

The first step in healing this is to slow down and recognise the role we have played out in life. We are not responsible for everyone's needs, but we are responsible for our own. It takes time to become aware of these stories and beliefs we have held on to tightly. Each day, like the crow, we will have to let go of our old ways and begin to pull twigs off the tree that will support our authenticity and create strong new foundations. Over time, this will awaken our true purpose in the world.

In an ongoing practice of stillness, we will recognise the stories we have told ourselves and finally give ourselves permission to nurture and care for our own needs. When we change this in ourselves, trust me, we do this for all the generations to come.

Questions to ask in Stillness

Find a quiet place to sit with your journal and ask yourself the following questions. You may like to draw or paint any associated feelings that arise:

What is the first thing I do when I hear that someone needs help?
What is the first thing I do when I need something?
Do I take the time to listen to or nurture my needs?
Do I take responsibility when life is difficult?
What role was I given as a child?
Do I see how this has continued into adulthood?
What do I want to change?
How would I do this?

An exercise for those taking on too much responsibility

Take some time and make a list of all things you 'think' you are responsible for in life.

Go through each responsibility on this list and ask, 'Am I responsible for this?' Answer honestly.

How do you feel when you let go of a responsibility on the list?

Who are you if you are not responsible for everyone and everything?

Responsibility

Does this leave you with more time to take care of yourself and your needs?

Do you feel comfortable taking responsibility for yourself? If not, why?

Make a list of how you schedule your day to be more responsible for yourself and less of others.

An exercise for those not taking responsibility in life

Take some time to make a list of all the things you 'think' you are responsible for in life.

Growing up, did someone in your family take responsibility for your needs?

Has this continued into adulthood?

What makes you believe you cannot do this by yourself?

How do you feel when someone takes responsibility for you?

Do you like this feeling?

What do you need to do to gain the skills to change this and the courage to do more?

What would change in your life if you took responsibility for yourself?

Universal Languages

*Laughter, love, grief and music are all universal
languages of the heart.*

One day, out in nature, I was watching two birds on a branch. I noticed how intensely they were chirping at each other, and at one stage I thought they might attack. However, as I patiently continued watching, I realised they were just chatting in their own language!

As I walked home, I reflected on how each of us express ourselves uniquely in the world. I realised that when someone is expressing themselves in a way that is unfamiliar to us, we may be quick to judge or separate from them, when in fact we just don't understand them.

They may be expressing their unique language through their clothing, hair and music, or their words or mannerisms. Either way, what matters is not how they are doing it, but understanding 'why' they are doing it.

One movie that I will never forget is *Babel*[20], which powerfully portrays the diversity of our communication around the world. *Babel* weaves stories from Morocco, America, Mexico and Japan, and shows us how one choice changed the lives of many people. Yet, this experience was communicated so differently around the world, depending on the perspective and the culture.

When we separate from another because we do not understand them, it is only because of our fear of the unfamiliar. However, when we take the time to learn a unique language or style of communicating from another, over time we will bridge the gap between us, and this will create more harmony and peace in our world. In the end, no matter what part of the world we come from, or the cultural background or beliefs we were born into, we all have a right to be heard, validated and taken care of.

Often the reason we feel separated from a family member, work colleague or partner is because we have not understood their style of communicating or their love language. Each of us has learned a unique way to express our love and communication to another. This will be different for everyone and is based on our childhood experiences, cultural beliefs and the role models we had growing up.

Unfortunately, often we believe that our way of expressing love or our view of the world is the only way to communicate. When our partner or someone around us expresses this in another way, we may believe they are wrong and we are right, but this attitude only creates more barriers between us. In this space, no one receives what they need.

Universal Languages

To understand this more deeply, it is helpful to know the five languages of love: words of affirmation, quality time, receiving gifts, acts of service and physical touch.[21]

Our partner's love language might be 'physical touch' or 'words of affirmation'. Either way, when we take the time to notice the unique style of communication or patterns in our loved ones, we can find creative ways to respond to this. In doing so, they will respond to us more positively and will begin to honour the way we communicate in the world.

Taking the time to say, 'Thank you' or 'I appreciate what you do in our family' can not only change someone's energy for the day but will affect our energy when they respond to us in a positive way. When we take a moment to give a gentle hug to our children or take the time to listen and ask what they need, it validates them and allows them to communicate more openly with us.

Some people like receiving gifts, but this does not mean we need to buy something for them every day. Often my husband will leave a little note at my computer or in another thoughtful space that reminds me he loves me. This is a simple but powerful message to our partners that we care about them, and this makes all the difference.

The truth is if we want to be understood, we do not need to learn a new language, but rather take the time to learn about one another and be patient as we discover the best form of communication between us.

Perhaps, if it is too difficult to share openly about our feelings, we can write a letter, a song, a poem, or make a video for someone we care about. The more we know ourselves and what we need to work on, the more we will know the person we want to communicate with and the more likely we will come up with something that will speak to them.

When we feel heard and understood, we feel a deep connection with all life, and over time we learn to pull down the barriers and the wounds that separate us from love, connection and receiving.

Questions to ask in Stillness

Find a quiet place to sit with your journal and ask yourself the following questions. You may like to draw or paint any associated feelings that arise:

How do I communicate with others in the workplace or at home?
Are there are barriers between myself and others?
Do I feel listened to?
If not, how does this make me feel?
Could I find another way to express my needs?
Do I need to understand their love language or the way they communicate? What creative ideas could I come up with to do this?
How would they respond if they felt listened to or validated?

Our Health

When we prioritise our health, we prioritise the sacredness of all life.

As a child, I was often sick. Sick with a sore throat, a cough or a pain somewhere in my body. And one time, I even thought I swallowed a pin and was rushed up to the hospital for an X-ray, only to find that nothing was there.

Looking back, I can now see it was just a cry to be seen and heard. I did not do this consciously; rather, I developed a behavioural pattern that was rewarded with attention from my parents.

This is also why so many children or adults unconsciously use sickness as a form of receiving attention or nurturing from others. Growing up, we may not have learned how to nurture ourselves or ask for support, so often we wait until we are sick and then believe we are worthy of attention.

Our body has an amazing intelligence that lets us know what we need way before we are aware of it. Each physical symptom I developed had been preceded by my thoughts, my feelings or from the experiences I had. And by this, I mean if I had been feeling rejected or left alone as a child, the next day, I might have had a sore throat or a pain in my stomach.

No matter if we have a toothache or have just been diagnosed with cancer, it is our body's only way to communicate with us when we are not listening or understanding our soul's higher purpose. Our unconscious body also contains our unprocessed pain from the past. So, if our body speaks, we need to listen.

When we do not listen to the whisper, the body will increase the volume until it gets our attention. Our body never lies, so even though we may say to others, 'I feel great', our body may be showing us a completely different story. Our body's only purpose is to live out our deepest purpose and potential in life and so, if we are moving away from this, our body we make sure we know it.

The health of our immune system is significantly impacted by several factors: our emotional state, our level of stress, our belief system and our nutritional input.

Even though our body's natural state is a state of well-being, it knows when we are not aligned or when we are not living in our truth, and it never lets us down. How often have we ignored a nagging pain in our back, in our shoulder, or in our body, only to discover later that we need months of rehabilitation and time to recover.

Or how often have we felt the first signs of a virus or sickness in our body and completely shut down the thought that this is a signal from our body to listen, nurture and understand. Instead, we do everything possible to control or reject this in us, avoiding the lesson and the opportunity to heal deeply.

Between prescription use, alcohol use and our addiction to the internet, we have plenty of ways to distract ourselves and block the messages that our body is trying to give us. However, when we do acknowledge our physical symptoms, we might respond with a learned mantra, like 'You will be fine', or 'Don't be so dramatic', or 'Solider on'.

To understand why we ignore or dismiss the signs and symptoms that our body gives us, we first need to understand our beliefs and thoughts around sickness and nurturing.

Take yourself back to childhood. What memories or experiences did you have when you were sick? How did your parents react when you were sick? Did they nurture you? Were they too busy to notice? Did they dismiss your symptoms? Did they exaggerate your symptoms? How did your parents respond to their wellbeing when they were sick?

Once we have a clear vision and understanding of our childhood experiences, we can start to piece together why we respond the way we do to ourselves or others when we are unwell. Neuroscience suggests that the more emotions and conflicts we experienced growing up, the more anxiety or physical symptoms we may feel later in life. Our goal is not to resist stress or ignore it, but rather befriend it and work with it.

Through my meditation practice and stillness in nature, I learned that when my body was relaxed and connected to higher vibrations, it naturally healed itself. But when I was stressed, disconnected or busy in life, it took much longer to recover.

When people are asked what is most important to them, the number one answer is always their health. Health problems, even minor ones, can interfere and overshadow every aspect of our life, and over time take a toll on our happiness and mental health. Our wellbeing is essential if we want to have more time and energy to do the things we want in life.

When we become familiar with our body and feel where we are holding tension or stress, we learn to listen to its messages. From here, we begin to make the right choices for our needs and create practices that support and nurture good health. Nurturing this intuition takes time and a daily practice. However, over time this helps us become clear on what will nourish our souls and empower us to choose from a place of love and not fear.

Often it is only when we slow down or go on holiday that our body has an opportunity to reveal the enormous toll it has taken due to our long-term chronic stress and busyness. Often it is on these very holidays or time away we may find a lump in our breast or finally address the chronic pain we had been ignoring or sedating. While we are running around, we often miss vital messages that our body is sending us and wanting to address in us.

When a tragic diagnosis is given to us, it may wake us up to live a healthier life. But unless we acknowledge and address our unconscious beliefs and patterns that influence our daily choices and unless we recognise how we are speaking to ourselves, it is only a matter of time before we are led back to the familiar habits that created our diagnosis in the first place.

Introducing discipline and healthier life choices are the first steps towards healing. Healing our unconscious beliefs and behavioural patterns takes patience and practice. It requires a new vision and direction than the one we learned growing up. It requires us to change our response to life and to move away from the familiar and into our fear of the unknown.

It's important to note that it is not just stillness we need for good health, but also movement. Our modern lifestyle at work and home, and out socially, can often be sedentary, which does not allow space to move out our old energy and allow new energy in.

Jon Kabat-Zinn, an American professor of medicine and the creator of the Stress Reduction Clinic and the Centre for Mindfulness, began seeing patients with chronic disease in the basement of his medical centre almost forty years ago.

His hypothesis was simple: the practice of mindfulness could help alleviate the pain and suffering associated with chronic disease, and thanks to his disciplined work and studies, we now understand that mindfulness not only reduces pain and suffering but can act as a preventative measure to reduce the incidence of stress-related illnesses.[22]

Each day, we choose how we think, act, exercise, and what we eat and drink. Each choice creates a platform for our wellbeing. Each morning, we get to begin again.

Often we do not create the right disciplines or choices towards optimum health because we were not nurtured as children. This can lead to habits in adulthood where we do not know how to slow down and take care of ourselves. On an unconscious level, we may believe we are not worthy for our body to receive the love and attention it needs. Instead, we disconnect and ignore the signs that our body is giving us.

Of course, another way we can avoid taking responsibility for our wellbeing is by allowing the medical system or friends and family to take this responsibility instead. Rather than listening to and nurturing our body, or taking the necessary steps towards wellbeing, we ignore the signs. Over time, this creates a great deal of pressure and responsibility on everyone around us.

Imagine a world where each of us took the time to be responsible for our body, mind and spirit? Like me, once I understood the emotional factor behind why I was always getting sick in my childhood, I learned to heal this wound and allow wellbeing to be a normal state in life.

When we feel run down or unwell, the first step we should take is to slow down and to question what is going

Our Health

on, what needs attention and why my body is sending me this message.

Pain in our body is simply a block in the flow and communication with life. For example, we may suddenly put our back out and convince ourselves it will be fine. However, if this keeps happening over a long period of time, we need to step back and question what is going on in us. Question the emotions behind it and the trauma stored in this part of our body.

For me, each time my body speaks to me, whether it is a headache or pain, I now understand it is an opportunity to stop and listen. And with practice, my health improved, my stress levels lowered, and this gave me freedom to do more in my life.

When we are unwilling to feel our guilt, our grief, or our trauma from the past, our body does not release these emotions over time; it stores this in our body's memory. At some point, when our body can no longer hold on to this build-up of energy, when we least expect it, it may present as a disease, a panic attack, depression or pain.

Often the habit of our mind is to disconnect from our suffering. Growing up, we may have learned to reject or to shut down when we did not like what we were feeling. We may have learned that feeling bad or vulnerable is a sign of weakness, and to be accepted by others, we should always feel great.

What I have discovered in many of my clients and myself is that when we ignore our pain and discomfort or reject our vulnerability, we use up more energy trying to disassociate from this rather than acknowledging and nurturing it.

The first step is to notice how quickly we want to disengage or distract ourselves from pain. When we reject a symptom, we are rejecting our deepest sense of nurturing and healing. To understand whether we do this or not, we need to become the observer of our symptoms and question our responses. What is our first response to pain? Do we nurture these messages or create busyness to avoid them? What do we need to do differently to prevent this from happening again?

For one week, observe and record how often you reach for a drink, food or substance when you feel stressed or experience pain in your body. Reviewing the results at the end of the week will help identify unhealthy patterns you may have developed unconsciously and reveal how a change in mood or challenging experience may trigger a self-destructive behaviour.

In the end, we can always find something more important than listening to and nurturing ourselves. However, if we do believe the most important aspect of our life is our health, then we need to follow up with the actions and disciplines that support this belief.

Creating a daily spiritual practice of yoga and stillness is my choice. It's here I feel and listen to the signs my body gives me. In doing so, I become more aware of my unconscious decisions and behaviours and learn to do the opposite.

I certainly don't always get it right, and there have been many times I have been out of balance. But that is why it is called a 'practice' because the next day, I choose again, and this makes all the difference to my wellbeing.

Questions to ask in Stillness

Find a quiet place to sit with your journal and ask yourself the following questions. You may like to draw or paint any associated feelings that arise:

What does healthy mean to me?
Do I feel comfortable being sick?
Was I nurtured as a child?
What benefits do I receive when I am unwell?
Do I feel comfortable nurturing myself?
If I am not responsible for my health, who is?
Could I take the time to nurture my needs and my health?
What new choices can I create to increase my wellbeing?

Moments of Resilience

Perseverance and resilience are born out of suffering.

Many times in life, I have based my decisions on fears or old beliefs, and this has always prevented me from experiencing growth. Statements like, 'Oh I couldn't never do that' or 'That's not my strength' were simply how I avoided my fears and from trusting I would be supported in life. I remember a beautiful lady from Compassionate Friends calling me one day after reading my book *Courage*. She loved it and asked me if I would give a talk at an upcoming grief seminar. My instant response was 'No sorry, I don't do public speaking.'

Fortunately, she did not back down, and together we explored why I was so quick to say no. In the end, she persuaded me to step up and find my courage to do something new. Speaking at this seminar opened so many doors for me and expanded a potential in me I did not know existed. To this day, I am grateful for her belief in me.

Learning to say 'yes' to life instead of saying 'yes' to our fears and insecurities allows us to live fully in this moment. Facing our fear of failure is never easy, but I have discovered many times that when I don't move beyond my fears and into the unknown, my creative gifts stay hidden, and I miss opportunities for growth.

When we are faced with trauma or difficult changes, often we feel helpless and cannot find the strength to go on. However, this is also the opportunity to discover our courage and resilience. Mother Earth is a beautiful example of this resilience and her ability to renew and restore herself again and again. We don't need to look far to see these regenerative powers in action. Mother Earth's profound potential to restore after bushfires, floods and drought are just a few examples that can teach us to do the same.

Looking back, I can see there were times after my son's death where I did not believe I had the resilience and strength to move forward. And yet, as I allowed myself to be vulnerable and lost in my grief, I discovered ways to move with it. I found the support I needed. I received the wisdom that led me to learn more about myself and found strength that I never knew I had. I learned to dig a little deeper each time, and every time, I found more courage and renewal.

In nature if we are dying of thirst and cannot see a water hole, it doesn't mean it is not there. It just means we need to dig deeper, persevere, and step by step, we will receive what we need.

Journalist Diane Coutu shares a story about Jim Collins, a teacher, author and advisor to business companies and social sectors. In this article she speaks about the interview

Jim had with a prisoner who was tortured by the Vietcong for eight years, and Jim will never forget the answer he received from one prisoner when he asked him who didn't make it out of the camps.

'Oh, that's easy,' said the prisoner. 'It was the optimists. They were the ones who said we would be out by Christmas. And then they said we would be out by Easter, and then by the by Fourth of July, and then out by Thanksgiving, and then it was Christmas again. They were the ones who kept avoiding the truth of their reality and the responsibility to change the situation they were in.' The prisoner then turned to Collins and said, 'You know, in the end, I think they all died of broken hearts.'[23]

Healing begins the moment we come to terms with our reality. This is not easy to do when we feel devastated or are facing a sudden tragedy. However, once we take some time to accept this difficult situation, we can surrender and allow support in. Often society encourages us to be optimistic in these situations or teaches us that being unmoved is a sign of resilience. However, this is not how I learned to heal.

Change and chaos insist we step out of the familiar and into a place of trust. They insist we adapt and move away from the old beliefs and stories and step into the unknown.

If there were no food or water in my current situation, I would understand that to survive, I must move. And so, it is the same with my suffering. When I know it is here, I have a choice: to stay and suffer, or move with it. And by moving with it, I mean moving with my reality and letting go of what I thought would happen. It means learning to adapt in this ever-changing moment. And being open and present to each step along the way.

Like Mother Nature, we all have the ability to persevere, thrive and adapt when given the space to do so. Knowing is not enough. In the end it will be our actions that create change. It will be our ability to stop, feel and allow life to support us along the way.

If you are thirsty right now or feel like you do not have the strength to go on, dig a little deeper. You have everything you need to do this. If I did, so will you. You will see, like the hidden waterhole in nature, it was waiting there all the time.

Questions to ask in Stillness

Find a quiet place to sit with your journal and ask yourself the following questions. You may like to draw or paint any associated feelings that arise:

What changes do I want in my life right now?
Do I believe I have the resilience to achieve them?
Do I need to dig a little deeper to discover my strength and courage?
How will I know if I do not step out into the unknown?
Do I trust in life?
Am I open to receive?
Am I ready to take responsibility and commit to these changes?

Part Four—Possibilities

Gateway to our Senses

To heal our trauma, we must learn to listen to and strengthen our senses and intuition.

After hearing the car hit my son's body in 2001, I had no idea that this trauma would stay locked within my body's memory. After this traumatic experience, each time I heard a loud bang or a car door slam, my body would react as if I were at the scene of the accident again.

In times of war, trauma or shock, we can be left with a physical imprint of our experience. The shock of this trauma interrupts our memory process and then stores the sound, feeling, smell or taste in our brain. When we become aware of our emotions and the sensations that arise from our external and internal experiences, we learn to understand what we need. We learn to trust whether we need to stop and slow down or move away and protect ourselves.

Our five senses – sight, hearing, touch, taste and smell – although seeming to operate independently, in reality, work as one. Our senses communicate information about our environment, which then determines how we perceive our world. This perception is vital to our survival and is our intuitive guide to detect danger and harm. However, after trauma, our perception can be distorted, and we can be triggered by a sound or a feeling that isn't a threat in our present moment, or won't result in the same experience we had before.

Everything that we consume in life is through our senses: touch, sight, hearing, smell and taste. Each one influences our mind and our behaviour. What we eat, what we speak and what we think all feeds our mind and our response to life.

Research in this area has found that sound, touch and sight are inextricably connected.[24] For example, if we lose our sense of taste or our sense of smell, all the other senses are affected and compromised. This proves that when we are aligned and at one with life, our senses are heightened and work well together.

However, because of childhood experiences or ancestral wounds, the reality for most of us is that our intuition has been clouded in fear, anger or distrust. Over time, this prevents us from tuning into our senses more clearly or developing healthy perspectives in life. Our perspective is the lens through which we see life. If we have been traumatised growing up, we may see life through a lens of distrust, injustice and or scarcity. Of course, we do this unconsciously, so it's important to be patient as we become aware of these behaviours in us.

In this unconscious state, we may choose unhealthy behavioural patterns, which can lead us to suffering. Finding practitioners that can help shift these wounds in our body's memory is the first step, and then a daily practice to change our thoughts and actions.

Peter Levine in his book *Trauma and Memory* says our 'traumatic memories are fixed and static and they do not yield to change, nor do they readily update current information. These memories, over time, tend to rise in us as fragmented splinters of emotions, images and smells.'[25]

This means if we are holding trauma in our body memory and do not move this energy through somatic healing (*healing and moving trauma out of our body*) or return these separated parts of us that are lost during trauma, we will continue to be triggered by the memories of smell, sound or images associated with this trauma. In doing so, we will not see or feel the fullness in every moment.

Part of healing our senses after trauma is to set healthy boundaries that protect us in life. These boundaries can be difficult to create, especially when we are overwhelmed with feelings of fear, obligation or guilt. For example, we may have to ask our parents or friends to stop giving us advice or to give us space to create change. We may have to stop seeing people that influence our behaviours in unhealthy ways. Change is never easy; however, each day, one step at a time, it is possible.

Creating time to strengthen our intuition is the next step. When was the last time you made a decision based on your intuition or a gut feeling? Intuition is like a muscle in our body and the more we tune into each day, the stronger it will become. As we learn to listen and become aware of our senses, a gateway of wisdom will open, and this will lead us into our authentic truth. When this becomes a practice for life, it will eliminate our exposure to trauma and suffering.

Ledi Sayadaw, one of the great Burmese meditation masters and scholars of the late nineteenth and early twentieth centuries, likened our senses to six train stations, from which the trains travel to various destinations. Each train can either take us to the stations of suffering and pain, or can take us to realms of happiness, freedom and awakening. [26]

Making the right decisions in life happens each time we create silence and listen. We cannot tune into our senses when we feel overwhelmed, busy or stressed. We cannot receive wisdom or new perspectives when we are still holding on to deep wounds or using a lens of suffering. Creating a practice to focus and tune into our intuition and senses is how we strengthen our insights. These insights help us make better decisions and help us live out our soul's purpose.

Each sense we have is a gift, and learning to recognise each one can help us expand these gifts:

My ears – I move into a place of stillness. I close my eyes to enhance my hearing. I observe the sounds that come and go without interpretation or judgement. I listen for the messages and sounds of insight.

My eyes – When I am outside, I take in all the colours, lights and shadows that life and nature create. I also take time to close my eyes and sit in darkness to reflect the contrast. I am grateful for the gift of sight.

My nose – I focus on my sense of fragrance with my food, in nature and in my home. I become aware of the different smells and how my body responds to each.

My tongue – I close my eyes to heighten my sense of taste. I note the sensations my tongue creates with each type of food or beverage I taste. I am grateful for my sense of taste and the experiences it creates.

My body – I focus and feel different textures and objects in my hand, one at time. I connect to the feelings this creates in my body or my memory. I focus on each part of my body and sense how each part feels.

My mind – I create a place of stillness and focus on my breath. In this space, I become aware of my thoughts and the stories they tell. I allow my thoughts to be here and notice how often they pull me away from being and into doing. I use my breath to slow down my thoughts and to focus on this moment. I note how peaceful my mind feels after I sit in stillness.

When I take the time to observe my senses, I understand which ones are blocked and which ones need nurturing.

I still may jump from time to time when I hear a loud noise, but now I remember that I am safe and that I am here, present to the fullness of life. In this space, I become aware of the signals, messages and the intuition that life offers me.

Questions to ask in Stillness

Find a quiet place to sit with your journal and ask yourself the following questions. You may like to draw or paint any associated feelings that arise:

Please scan your body slowly, from the top of your head to the bottom of your feet and ask yourself:
What sensations do I feel in my head, shoulders, arms, heart, abdomen, legs and feet?
What do I see?
What do I hear?
What feels blocked or heavy in my body?
What feels light and easy in my body?

Now focus on your heart space:
How do I feel about myself and my life at present?
What emotions are coming to the surface when I ask this question?
Do I need to breathe out and nurture these feelings?
Do I need to rest and restore my energy?

Sacred Moments

When I recognise the sacred in this moment, the sacred is seen in every part of life.

I have learned many times over that being alive and healthy is the most sacred gift I can have in life, and each time I choose to be present, the sacred is seen.

I choose activities and experiences that reflect this sacredness. I choose foods that honour my body. I choose experiences and activities that I know will open my energy and allow life to flow through me. I offer daily gratitude for all the abundance in my life. When life is challenging, or I feel overwhelmed, I step back and practise ceremony, honouring my feelings.

Creating simple and sacred moments does not need to be time-consuming or difficult. In fact, once I started a practice, I began to see how simple it was.

Of course, even if we choose one or two mindful practices a day or once a week, it all contributes to an increase in energy and a deeper connection with life. Some days, I fill a jug of water in the morning. I add some slices of lemon, then I place my hand over the jug and I thank Mother Earth for this life-filled source of water energy. Throughout the day as I pour the water in my glass, I am grateful for each mouthful and for the gift of clean water.

Some of the practices I try to do during the week can include pausing before I eat or placing my hand over my food and offering a prayer of gratitude. If it is fish, I thank the fish for its life and for the energy I am receiving. Sometimes if I am eating alone, I am present to each mouthful of food and the abundance before me. Some days I watch myself jump into conversations and say too much, and on other days I pause before I speak or before I give advice.

When I exercise outside or inside, I practise being aware of everything around me. When I am in nature, I notice the sky above me, the trees, and the earth below me. I honour the earth I walk on and sit on. In this place, I am more present to the signals and messages I receive.

One practice I have started and like to share with friends is a sacred tea ceremony. First, I light a candle and then create mindful steps to make the tea. Each part of the process is mindful and slow. And as the tea settles in the pot, we take the time to share what we are grateful for and then we pour the tea and enjoy this time together.

A sacred ritual we can do at home is to create a sacred space in one of our rooms. Most of us have a quiet room or corner in our home that we feel relaxed and comfortable in. It can be near a window where the sunlight beams through and warms our energy or in the corner of our favourite bedroom.

In this room, we can place a candle, some flowers, incense or Palo Santo wood, and this can be placed on an altar or a box covered with material or on a windowsill. Being creative in this space is part of the process to create sacred moments in our life.

Once set up, we can take some time to light a candle, practise a short meditation or breathing exercise and perhaps journal our thoughts, insights or ideas and intentions for the future. Over time, this space becomes sacred and each time we allow ourselves to 'be', we move back into the flow and fullness of this moment. In this space, we can listen deeply and receive.

Another activity we can do to create sacred understanding is to be creative and open. The unconscious mind is not only where we find our wounding, but where we hold our blueprint or soul purpose in life. Creating art and collages, or painting and drawing, is one way to express and discover this within us. Set up some art materials in a quiet environment. Before you start, set an intention or a question that you would like to be answered through your art.

Allow yourself to explore this expression freely, without worrying if it is right or wrong. There is no need to be good at art or painting to achieve this. Allow yourself to be vulnerable and open. Allow your intuition to guide you. After you have completed your painting, drawing or collage, take some time to step back and see the symbols or messages your unconscious mind has shown you. Ask yourself, 'What do I feel when I see these symbols or colours? 'What messages are awakening in me when I look at this art?' Write down the messages that have been given to you.

Another idea to create a space for our wellbeing is to give ourselves a foot spa at home. This is an easy way to rejuvenate and ground our energy, but more importantly take care of our feet, which are often neglected. After filling a bowl with warm water, we can add essential oils of peppermint, lavender or rosemary. If our feet are tired, we can add Epsom salts. Then to create ambience, we can light a candle and play relaxing music in the background. As we allow this sacred time for ourselves, we can remember what it feels like to be nurtured and to make this a priority.

There are so many creative ways we can become aware of what is sacred in our life and to nurture our wellbeing. Each time we become mindful in our day-to-day actions, we become one with life. We become aware of how precious time is and how important it is to honour every moment we are given.

Questions to ask in Stillness

Find a quiet place to sit with your journal and ask yourself the following questions. You may like to draw or paint any associated feelings that arise:

How can I create sacred moments in my life?
When would I do this?
Do I allow time for myself to be grateful and mindful?
What stops me from allowing this?
Where in my day can I make time to nurture the sacred moments in life?
How often would I do this in my week?

*

*When I take the time to nurture my body
I become aware of my needs.
In this space
I remember to listen and receive.
In this space I rejuvenate my energy.
In the silence, I remember what is sacred.*

Dreaming Moments

Our dreams are messages and guides that can lead us to clarity and wisdom in life.

Not long after our son's funeral, I began to have very vivid dreams. I dreamed about the car accident, the hospital, and on other occasions, I would dream of Nathan hugging and kissing me and reminding me that he loved me. Over time, I discovered that my dreams were messengers, and this created a deeper understanding of my life and my future. Many years later, and after I had established a strong meditation practice, I began to have psychic dreams about my future and about others' futures as well.

Carl Jung, a Swiss psychiatrist, saw dreams as the psyche's attempt to communicate important things to the individual. He valued dreams highly, and perhaps above all else, as a way of knowing what was really going on. Marie-Louise von Franz, a scholarly colleague of Jung's, wrote, 'Dreams are the voice of nature within us and are the sacred place where human and cosmos meet and interact.'[27]

While some of us may not remember our dreams, it is thought that we dream between three to six times a night and that these dreams can last between five to twenty minutes. Some scientists speculate that the purpose of dreaming may not be psychological but physiological. Rapid-eye movement or REM sleep has been thought to help the brain process memories and trauma.[28]

As I have learned to remember my dreams every night, I am now aware of their importance in my waking life and the warnings they may have for me.

Over the years, I have had many dreams, but some of the common ones have been about houses. The house represents 'the self' and the reflection of the house in our dream is the view we have about ourselves in our waking life.

For example, in one of my dreams I was in a large, beautiful and expansive home, but at the back of the home there was a big room that was being renovated (the back of the house representing the past). And as I was walking through the back of the house, I remembered feeling disappointed about how long the renovations were taking and realising how much there was left to do.

Upon waking, I took the time to reflect on this dream and realised this was a beautiful reflection on what was happening in my waking life. At the time, I was going through some significant changes and healing from my past, and I was impatient with how long it was taking. However, what I also remembered was that the house in my dream was expansive and beautiful, and over time, so would I be.

In our dreams, the size of the house or where our home is located can reflect how we feel about ourselves or our living situation. To see an attic that is dark and has lots of furniture and old boxes could represent hidden memories or repressed thoughts. If the attic is bright and clear, it may symbolise a clear open mind and our connection to our higher self.

One of the dreams I have had is being surrounded by water or the ocean. The symbolism of water in our dreams can represent our deep and unconscious emotions. When I dream about being overwhelmed by water, I find a few days later I will experience these emotions in my waking life. Water dreams can represent a part of us that needs to be acknowledged, nurtured and released, and in doing so, we allow transformation and renewal.

In the end, our dreams are a gift to understand and help guide us in our waking life.

So how do we remember our dreams?

While most of us remember one or two dreams a week, there are some people who say they never dream. However, we all dream; the only difference is that some of us don't remember them in the morning. If we want to remember the messages that our unconscious mind is sending us, we must be willing to slow down our busy minds. In my own experience, it was my daily meditation and stillness practice that greatly increased my ability to remember my dreams and to interpret the messages I was given. This makes sense, because if I am busy and stressed in my waking life, my mind is easily distracted, and this will make it harder to settle into a deep sleep and remember the messages in the morning.

If we knew how important our dreams were to our waking life or knew how our dreams could pre-warn us about a serious health issue or an emotional turmoil in the future, we may feel more motivated to slow down, meditate and listen more deeply.

How to remember our dreams

A daily practice of meditation and stillness in nature will heighten our awareness, calm our minds and open our energy to see more deeply and to dream more clearly.

Before we go to sleep, we can take a few moments to set an intention that we will remember our dreams and have a journal near our bed to write them down. If we wake up after we have had a dream, this is a good time to write it down so we don't forget it in the morning. With practice, we will eventually stop having to write them down. It's also important to remember to stay off social media in the bedroom, making our room internet and phone free. The less distractions we have in our room, the deeper we will sleep.

No matter what we dream, whether it is a reunion with a loved one, a nightmare, a warning about our health or something strange, take the time to question these dreams and look up the meaning and interpretations of them. A recurring dream may be sending us a message that could save our life, so never underestimate the signals they have for us.

Our dreams are a gift and when we understand how to work with them, we can find solutions and creative insights in every part of our life.

Goal Setting

Our goals can only be achieved with a plan, passion and commitment.

I have always been fascinated by the endurance of marathon runners and their ability to stay focused on long distances. They say the race teaches them to dig deep, find their resilience and their ability to succeed. And so, I met with a marathon runner and asked him how he prepares for a marathon.

I asked, 'What intentions or disciplines do you practise before you run a marathon?'

He replied, 'Well, besides training each day and setting intentions, on the day of the race, I break my marathon down into five-kilometre goals.'

The runner said he felt confident he can run five kilometres, and so, his focus is only on that one goal, rather than on completing the entire marathon.

After he completes the five kilometres, he slows down, drinks water and re-focuses on the next five kilometres. And before he knows it, he has completed the marathon.

His approach inspired me to remember that when we break our goals down into small achievable steps, anything is possible.

Often the reason we do not complete our goals is because we have created a goal or vision that feels too overwhelming or too big for us to conquer. For example, 'equal rights' or 'world peace'. However, when we break it down into small steps and only focus on completing one step at a time, we will feel rewarded more often. Over time, this will motivate us, increase our confidence and expand our vision and goals in the future.

When we begin from where we are and do what we can now, we will find that this is more than enough. Sometimes in the face of change, we may not know where to begin. And so, we start small, and this can be giving someone a smile or a hug. This can be donating our clothes to charity or offering a neighbour a hand. When we create small circles of kindness, care and love in the world, over time this ripples out into wider circles, and this is what makes all the difference.

When it comes to goal setting, it's important to set an intention first. Often, we are told to 'Vision our goals' or 'Make it happen' or become the 'Co-creators of life'. However, in my experience, sometimes when we want to achieve something, our ego-mind takes over. This can lead us into believing we know exactly how and when this will happen. When we are led by our intuition and with an open mind, we are much more likely to be led on the right pathway.

Goal Setting

Therefore, before I even set a goal or vision for the future, I start by sitting quietly and asking, 'Is this coming from my 'heart space', which is my inner knowing and intuition, or my 'ego'.

Goals are often directed by our ego or from the conscious part of our mind that contains our thoughts, memories and emotions. Whereas a heart intention is where we will find our deep longing and soul purpose. Which not only helps us but others along the way.

For example, when I first decided to write this book, I was excited and felt a deep calling within. Each day I took the time to be guided by my intuition and spirit, and to understand what needed to be shared in this book. However, an example of being in my ego-mind is when I have felt the need to go and make something happen. Or felt I had to do something for someone else. And even when it was not flowing easily, I continued to believe I was right, and the universe was wrong! In these spaces, I always felt tired, impatient and irritated about my project.

'Intention' is a Latin word that means 'stretching and purpose'. To create an intention, I spend time in stillness and allow myself to listen and feel what is going on within me. I ask questions and have learned how to let my body respond, not my mind. Please know, it takes time to develop this.

Once I have asked the question, I wait to see if my body contracts and feels tight or if it feels easy and open. It takes practice, but my body never lies, whereas my mind often leads me astray. I write my intention out on a piece of paper, breathe it out into the world to be seen, and place it on my altar as a first step towards manifestation.

I then take some time to write down my ideas and understand what needs to be done. I ask, 'Do I need support to achieve this?' 'What daily actions do I need to set in place to complete this goal?' I continue to ask questions and to develop a clearer picture of my goal and the pathway ahead.

I do not worry how or when this intention will manifest; I just keep moving towards the next guided step. It took me a long time to trust in this process. But each time I practised stillness, I was always given a message or a signal that guided me. In doing this, I also allowed more time to do the things I love and to be present with my family and friends.

Another way to achieve a goal is to 'envision'. Vision is a Latin word meaning 'to see' or to 'vision into the future'. Visioning our ideas, dreams or passions can help manifest this into our reality. To keep our vision alive, there are a few ways we can do this. We can picture ourselves completing our goal and imagining our excitement and happiness. We can picture everyone around us congratulating us at the end and supporting our vision. We can imagine that the path to this goal is easy and that we have everything we need to complete it. Just be careful when doing this that we do not create visions based on our ego-mind, which can lead us into illusions and disappointment.

When we feel safe to live in the uncertainty of life and in this present moment, we are much more likely to feel our intuition and the signs life gives us. In this space, we remain open to all the opportunities and possibilities in life, and may be surprised how much there is to receive.

It only takes one decision, one idea and a new perspective to change our destiny. Always start small and from where you are. With patience, courage and focus, anything is possible.

Questions to ask in Stillness

Create some time and space to focus on your needs. Have a journal, pen or art supplies ready. Close your eyes and take some deep breaths in and out. Relax your body. Breathe in and out deeply and write down three goals/intentions you wish to achieve or receive. Then ask:

Is this coming from my intuition or ego-mind?
Take some time to feel the answers in your body, rather than listen to your thoughts.
What steps can I take each day which will help me align with my truth and become aware of the signs that life gives me?
Am I ready to accept the sacrifice and discipline that this will take?
What practices will help me listen to my senses and my intuition?
What support do I need to achieve this goal?
What intentions can I set today?

A Simple Life

Become empty so that you can be filled.

When our family moved to Italy in 2007, we had no idea how much it would change our life. In my first book *Courage* I shared how we received a sum of insurance money after the death of our son. And in between that time, we had another beautiful daughter named April.

It took us some time to know what we wanted to do with this money. Although it was not a great deal of money, we wanted to spend every cent on something that was meaningful and would honour Nathan and his precious life. We realised we all loved the Italian culture; we loved their food, their language and their country. However, after six years of living with our grief, we also felt we needed space and a new environment to go within and heal deeply.

Leaving our jobs, renting out our home and moving the girls away from their schools, family and friends was a big task and took courage from us all. And yet, as we stepped out into the unknown, we knew this was the right decision.

Living simply is learning that even when we have nothing around us, we still have everything within. It's about finding balance in our work and day-to-day life. It's about finding space to align our energy in vibrations that are expansive and nurture our mind, body and spirit.

It is about paring back and living in the fullness of 'what is' already here, rather than what 'might be' in the future. It's about creating spaces to breathe and re-connect to the beauty and abundance in this moment.

In Panzano, a small village in Tuscany, we lived a simple life. We had a limited budget, so we learned to be creative with what we did have. We found joy and learned patience in the simple moments, like making our own bread or pasta. Or walking through the village and taking the time to meet new people and understand the Italian culture. Sometimes, just getting gelato in town, although simple, felt abundant.

Our host, who lived next door to us in Panzano, grew all her own vegetables and food. She had olive trees, and every animal she raised and eventually ate was always done in a mindful manner. She taught us to appreciate everything we had and to be patient as the produce grew. In Italy we asked, 'What is important in our life?' After losing Nathan, our priorities, our future and our goals had changed forever. We now took the time to be present with each other. We now took the time to live fully in each moving moment.

A Simple Life

Hans Christian Andersen reminds us that 'the whole world is a series of miracles, but we're so used to them, we call them ordinary things.'[29]

Living simply does not mean living without. It means taking the time to understand and notice the miracles in every part of our life and learn to create beautiful memories from them. When we simplified our life with the girls in Italy, we discovered what was precious and what we loved doing together. We realised we did not find this wisdom or understanding when we were busy, or when we were saying 'yes' to everything and everyone and 'no' to ourselves.

One of the many lessons I learned in Panzano was when I watched the Italians cook. For example, early in the morning they often made homemade bread, pasta, pastry or started a slow-cooked meal. I realised that because cooking was a priority to them, they simply adapted their day around making it happen. When I first saw someone bake bread early in the morning, I remember thinking, 'I would never consider doing this at home!' But the Italians taught me repeatedly that everything is possible when we prioritise what is important and precious to us.

Often, we vow to ourselves as young children or adults we will not follow in the footsteps of our parents or grandparents. But unless we slow down to feel and see the patterns we are carrying and living out for them, we may end up doing exactly what we vowed to do differently.

We can begin to simplify our life by looking around our home and the lifestyle we have created. Joshua Fields Millburn and Ryan Nicodemus were one of the first people to introduce minimalism to the western world. For Joshua, this transformation began in 2009 after his mother died and his marriage ended in the same month. It was during this tragic and difficult time that Joshua began to question his life and ask what he could let go of or where he could make room for more.[30]

Minimalism is all about keeping what adds value and meaning to our life and to those we love, and learning how to remove the rest. It's about becoming intentional with our time, relationships and what we own in life. Remembering because we only have a certain amount of energy and time in our day, we need to choose wisely what will make our life full or empty.

Like Joshua and Ryan, sometimes in our discontentment, or an experience with loss or death, it creates a search for meaning and questions our purpose and priorities in life. I wonder why it's not until we face a tragedy, lose our job or find out we are dying that we decide what is important to us. Or why we keep putting off our dreams for another day.

On an unconscious level, we may believe that bad things only happen to bad people, or that if we move fast enough, life will not catch up with us and reveal our fears, vulnerabilities and unworthiness.

Before Nathan died, I did not listen to or question my beliefs about life. I did not understand that fullness was felt by being still in each moment or that feeling grateful for what I already had created more abundance.

A Simple Life

Perhaps we can take a moment to ask, 'What can I let go of?' 'How will letting go create more room in my life?' 'Am I doing a job I love?' 'Where do I hope I will be in ten years' time?' 'What if a health issue arises and prevents me from doing what I have spent my whole life preparing for?' 'Am I in a relationship that is nurturing me and allowing me to grow?' 'Am I happy?'

When we ponder these questions and discover we are not where we are meant to be, then our next question might be, 'Why are we ignoring our freedom and happiness?'

It was only when I slowed down that I felt the restlessness in me and understood what I could let go of. I learned that living simply gave me so much more than a busy life. I learned it opened my mind to see the sacred in everyone and everything, and more importantly, it left no room for regrets.

I realised that when life was simple, I felt a deep connection with all life, but when I was busy and running around, I missed opportunities and the ability to find peace.

Perhaps the question we can contemplate is, 'Now that we have advanced technology in every part of our life and the labour-saving devices on hand to make life easier, has this decreased or increased our busyness? Has moving away from the old traditions and the wisdom of our First Nations elders increased or decreased our understanding of life? Has disconnecting from the earth to grow our own vegetables or fruit trees increased our ability to recognise our immense abundance or decreased our ability to over-consume?'

When we recognise how we connect with others and with life, we will find the answers to our suffering and our feelings of isolation. We may find that living simply and slowing down is the only way we will learn to re-connect to a deeper source of life and a deeper sense of self.

At the end of the day, what I have learned from slowing down and simplifying my life is summed up by the wisdom of Lao Tzu: 'Great trouble comes from not knowing what is enough. Great conflict arises from wanting too much. When we know when enough is enough, there will always be enough.'[31]

Questions to ask in Stillness

Find a quiet place to sit with your journal and ask yourself the following questions. You may like to draw or paint any associated feelings that arise:

Am I happy where I am right now?
What am I hoping will change so that my life improves?
Is this realistic?
What can I let go of to make room for nurturing and peace?
What is positive in my life right now?
How often are my thoughts in the future and not here in the present?
What can I do to change this?
How would simplifying my life help change my current situation?

Meditations – Stillness & Movement

Life is made up of stillness and movement.
To find a balance in these two states of being, we must learn to
listen deeply and practise both each day.

Stillness Meditations

A meditation for focus

Find a quiet place to sit outside.
Close your eyes.
Focus on your breath and take some deep, slow breaths in and out.
Relax your shoulders and your body with each exhale.
Feel your base chakra on the earth and feel its strength and support.
Open your eyes.
Now focus on something in nature or in the area you are in, perhaps a flower, plant, tree, animal or insect.

Notice the details with curiosity and notice how it moves in the world.
See this object with childlike wonder.
Take in all the details however small, however big.
Take some time to absorb this information.
Be grateful for the wisdom in the small aspects of life.
See the sacred in everyone and everything.

Morning ritual

I stand on my yoga mat.
I focus on my breath.
I move in and out and stretch into my yoga poses.
I breathe out old energy.
I breathe in new energy.
I finish renewed.
I move into my healing room.
I light a candle.
I open sacred space and call in the energy from the south, the north, the east and the west.
I burn my Palo Santo wood and as the sweet smoke spirals over my body and my room, I feel cleansed.
I honour my ancestors and pray for my family.
I sit in silence.
I listen deeply.
I open myself to receive wisdom and insights.
I receive this in gratitude.
I draw some oracle or tarot cards.
I receive these messages and I set my intention for the day.

A guided visualisation if you cannot be outside

Have a journal with you during this meditation in case you need to write down any insights or wisdom you receive.

Close your eyes, and slowly take some deep breaths in and out until you feel your body is relaxed. Once you feel settled, visualise you are walking barefoot in a beautiful, lush forest, and at the end of this forest is a large oak tree. Focus on walking towards this tree. Notice the fairy lights that are illuminating the pathway and feel the texture of the leaves and earth against your bare feet.

Now walk down the five steps that are in front of you. As you leisurely step down, breathe out slowly and release any heavy energy after each step. At the bottom of the stairs, you will see a beautiful landscape and a large oak tree in front of you. As you get closer to the oak tree, you will notice a small pillow to sit on. This pillow is filled with yellow and white energy, and as you sit gently down, feel this energy arise in you.

Now begin to visualise the sound of the river and the waterfall above you. Imagine hearing the birdlife more clearly and feel the aliveness and vitality of this environment.

Once you feel settled, set an intention to be shown what it is that you need to hear, feel or see in your meditation. Take some more deep breaths in and sit in silence as you wait and listen.

When you have received what you need and feel ready to finish, visualise standing up from your cushion and move away from the oak tree and towards the five steps. Move up each step separately and breathe in and out deeply until you reach the top. Feel yourself come back up to your present environment. Open your eyes. Thank your guides, who may have given you messages of wisdom, and write down any information you feel is important.

A meditation for expansion

Find a quiet place.
Take your time. There is no rush.
Sit for a few minutes, focusing on the sensation of your breathing, in and out.
Allow your thoughts to be here but continue to focus on your breath.
Close your eyes.
Visualise the expansive space of the blue sky.
Visualise the expansive land we live on.
Visualise the blue infinite ocean.
Focus on these spaces for a few minutes.
Feel this space within you.
Allow this expansive feeling to be here within you.
Notice what arises in you while you are in sitting in expansiveness.
It might be a physical discomfort, an emotion or an anxious thought. Allow it to be here, but keep focusing on the expansive energy around you.

Be with it all. Be compassionate to the story that is arising. You may feel disappointment or frustration, shame and anger. Allow.

Can you forgive those who have rejected you in the past?

Can you forgive yourself for rejecting these wounded parts of you?

Keep focusing on your breath in between.

Breathe out what feels uncomfortable. Breathe in to expand.

For the last few minutes, take time for self-compassion and releasing.

Affirmations

Today I focus on acceptance for myself and others.

Today I focus on expansive energy within me.

I move forward in loving compassion for myself and others.

I focus on what I can do and allow others to do the same.

I focus on gratitude and what I have.

I focus on love, and compassion.

Meditating in nature

Find a place in nature, in bushland, a forest, by a river or in a park.

As you walk slowly, honour the land you are on, and acknowledge the ancestors that have walked before you and honour their deep wisdom.

Be conscious and slow with every movement. As you touch each tree you see, imagine what this tree has seen or felt over the years. Imagine the stories this tree holds and the wisdom of the ages it can offer you. Be still, feel and listen.

Become present to the flowers, the plants and the animal life in the forest. Listen to their messages for you.

Keep focused on the environment you are walking through. Touch and connect to the rocks the river, the earth or anything you may feel drawn to.

Another way we can connect with a tree is to stand before one we feel drawn to and wrap our arms around its trunk. Make sure all your chakras on the front of your body are aligned and are open to the energy of this tree. Stay here for a few minutes and connect to the energy of this tree. Breathe in deeply.

Alternatively, you can sit at the base of the tree, with your back against the trunk of the tree, and imagine your body is growing roots from the base of your spine down into the earth. See these roots moving deeply into the ground, like the tree you are up against. Close your eyes and allow the energy of this tree to ground you and restore your energy.

Breathing slowly and deeply is important when you are meditating in nature. Take slow and long cleansing breaths in and out, releasing old energy out into the earth and breathe in clean, light energy.

Trees protect you, provide you with oxygen and create beautiful fruits and flowers. They are also the means to warm yourself in winter and to create fire for ceremony. And so, it makes sense that trees also encourage stillness and healing.

A breathing exercise to do at the river or ocean

Find a space in nature where there is water, either by a waterwall, the ocean, a creek or a river, or just close your eyes and imagine you are there.
Take some deep breaths in and out slowly, become aware of your surroundings.
Feel the earth underneath you, supporting you.
Acknowledge the ancestors of the land and your family ancestors and guides.
Allow your breath to pull you back into this moment and calm your thoughts.
As you breathe out, imagine your old energy and your breath are extending outwardly across the waters and into infinite space.
As you breathe in, imagine you are pulling this expansive light energy back into your energy field and body.
Repeat this five times.
Each time you breathe out, extend your breath and energy further out.
Each time you breathe in, draw in nature's infinite energy.
Notice how nature is creating this cycle naturally.
Breathe in life, breathe out what is no longer needed.
Breathe in new energy, release old energy.

Focus on the water flowing in and flowing out, without resistance.
Notice the moments in between the ebb and flow.
Notice and feel that space within you between breaths.
Trust in this natural rhythm of life.
Be here with it all.

A meditation for pain and suffering

Instead of struggling and resisting this moment, slow down and rest in the uncertainty. To live here is to be free. Take a moment to create some space for nurturing. No matter what is presenting in your body, there will always an emotion or an experience behind it, so unless you take the time to be with it and listen deeply to its message, it will continue to stay or return to you at another time.

Sit quietly outside in nature or in your room where you are resting.
Take some deep breaths in and out slowly.
Ask yourself, 'What am I feeling right now? Do I want to run or distract myself from this pain or feeling? Am I fearful of this pain or sickness?'
Just the question alone opens space in us.
Take a deep breath in and out again.
Imagine the pain in your body is a small child waiting to be heard or held.
What is this child asking of you?
Find compassion for this need within you.

Do you need to be nurtured, loved and taken care of?
Do you need support?
Do you feel comfortable asking for help?
Allow your feelings to arise, cry if you need to.
Sometimes just allowing and releasing can begin healing in your body.
Take some deep breaths in and out.
Journal your insights and thoughts if you need to.
At the end of your practice sleep, rest or ask for help.
Observe how your body feels after spending some time nurturing it.

A smiling gratitude meditation

Find a quiet space in nature or inside.
Take some deep breaths in and out.
Relax your body and your mind.
Relax your shoulders and your abdomen.
Relax your legs and your feet.
Focus on your feet.
As you are smiling, thank your feet for their support and strength.
As you are smiling, thank your legs for their ability to move and lead you in life.
As you are smiling, thank your hips and all the organs in your abdomen for their ability to nurture you and give you what you need.

As you are smiling, thank your stomach and the surrounding organs in the front and back of your body for digesting your food and keeping you healthy.
As you are smiling, thank your heart and your lungs for the gift of life.
As you are smiling, thank your shoulders, arms and hands for movement, support and the ability to create.
As you are smiling, thank your throat and your ability to express your authentic nature out in the world.
As you are smiling, thank your face for the ability to speak, to smell, to eat, to taste and to express your individuality out in the world.
As you are smiling thank your ears for listening, for all the sounds in life, for music, voices and nature.
As you are smiling, thank your eyes for their ability to see in life, for their perspective and the vision to understand.
As you are smiling, thank your mind, the intelligence of your brain and your ability to gain knowledge, wisdom and insight.

Star keeper and sky meditation

Life is always about balance. And even though we need to ground our energy on the earth, we also need meditations and ceremony that help us expand our thoughts and beliefs into the upper worlds. This helps us see life from a higher perspective.

Sometimes in life we can feel small and contracted, or we can feel miles away from the fullness of life. When we

Meditations: Stillness & Movement

open ourselves up to the energy above us, we can re-align and re-connect to our truth and expand this within us.

The sea, the mountains, the forests, the sky and the stars are all spaces that remind us we are part of this expansive and infinite space.

During the day, I focus on the sky and clouds, and if I am doing this at night, I focus on the stars or the moon.

Often the full moon is a beautiful space to do this meditation. Notice the stars and the planets. You can focus on the full moon or a constellation of stars. Focus on the beams of white light from these spaces and imagine this beam of light is moving towards your body.

Visualise a beam of light moving through the top of your head and slowly down each part of your body until it moves out of your feet. Breathe in this light-filled energy and breathe out and release anything that feels small or heavy in you. At the end of the meditation, send gratitude and love to the stars, sky and moon energy.

During the day, I lie back on the grass and connect to the expansive energy of sky and the warmth and strength of the sun's energy. I watch the clouds in constant movement and how they continually move into changing shapes, led by the wind.

I focus on the expansive blue of the sky and the strength and warmth of the sun and remember I too am a part of this beautiful energy. I visualise the sun's warm light energy moving through my body, which cleanses me and creates new perspectives in me. I use my breath to move this energy in and down my body and I breathe out and release anything that feels small and heavy in me. I feel the wind against my face and across my body and listen to any wisdom whispered to me in these spaces. I allow myself to let go and move out the energy I no longer need. I begin to feel this spaciousness arise in me again. I take the time to journal any thoughts and finish my practice outside. These are all practices I encourage you to do too.

Circle of Truth

When you feel stuck, overwhelmed or confused about a situation, you can create a ceremony to open your energy and listen deeply to your intuition.

You can create this circle inside your home or outside in nature and gather materials like flowers, petals, leaves, stones or sticks or anything that is available to make your circle.

Once completed, you sit in the circle.

Take some deep breaths in and out slowly.

Ask your guides, ancestors and higher beings to be with you.

Say to yourself, 'I am safe' and 'I am surrounded in love and in the circle of life'.

Ask your first question:

How do I feel?

This is the circle of truth, so fully express all that you are feeling, do not hold back.

Ask your second question:

What do I need?

Express exactly what you need in this moment, no matter if it's possible or not.
Ask your third question:
What steps can I take to shift out of this situation and move into the flow of life again?
Take your time to breathe, let go and open yourself to the answers and guidance that arises in the circle. Trust you will know what to do. Trust you will be supported in your decision.

Movement Meditations

Moving energy in and out of our body with our breath

Creating movement in our body each day is one way to release the dense energy that we accumulate. Yoga, exercise, massage and breathing exercises open our energy field. As we breathe and move out our heavy energy, we create space to feel, see and listen more deeply.

The deeper we dive into releasing this energy, the less likely we will be triggered by stress, anger and anxiety.

(1)
Sit in a comfortable quiet place; nature is best, but a quiet room is good too.
Begin by focusing on your breath. Focus on the rise and the fall of your chest with each breath.

Now take some deep breaths in slowly and out slowly.
Notice the difference between normal breathing and deep breathing.
Now breathe in deeply and hold for five seconds.
Breathe out and relax.
Repeat this five times.
Notice how your body feels after deep breathing.
Notice what happens to your heart rate as you breathe in and out slowly.
Notice how the breath relaxes you.
Now stand up.
Take a deep breath in and raise your arms up as you do this.
Just before you release your breath
Swing your arms down, bend your knees
And breathe out a loud 'HA' sound.
Release all the breath and energy in your body as you swing your arms down and breathe out 'HA'.
Repeat this three times.
(This helps release a build-up of energy in your body and invigorates your nervous system.)

(2)

Sit in a comfortable, quiet place.
Place one hand on your abdomen below your belly button and focus on this area.
Notice how your hand moves in with each inhale and moves out with each exhale.

Meditations: Stillness & Movement

Take some deep breaths in and out slowly, focusing on this movement.
Stay with this for three more breaths.
Imagine as you release your breath that any old energy is leaving your body through the base of your spine and into the earth.
Keep breathing out this energy into Mother Earth.
Notice how your body feels as you release this energy out of your body.
Repeat this three times.

(3)
Sit in a comfortable, quiet place.
Take some deep breaths in and out.
Now combine your breath with imagery and words that support relaxation.
Imagine the air you are inhaling as waves of peace and calm moving through your body.
Say to yourself as you inhale, 'I am inhaling peace and calm into my body'.
Now imagine the air you are exhaling is moving away your tension and anxiety.
Say to yourself as you exhale, 'I am exhaling tension and anxiety out of my body'.
You can change the words of affirmation each time you do this exercise.
Repeat this three times.

(4)
Sit either in nature or by a river.
Take your time to find a spot that you feel comfortable in.
Take some deep breaths in and out.
Become aware of the stillness in your surroundings.
Honour the ancestors of this land and your spirit guides.
Close your eyes.
Take some more deep breaths in and out.
What can you hear?
Spend some time listening deeply.
What can you feel?
Allow space to feel what is going on inside.
Open your eyes and ask, 'What can I see?'
Spend some time noting the signs of life around you and or any messages you are receiving in nature.

Affirmations
I am love
I am soul
I am light
I am infinite and abundant.

A walking meditation

A walking meditation is a combination of slow walking and pausing, which allows you to take in your environment and be present.

A walking meditation involves mindful and conscious steps and actions. At first, it will feel controlled or exaggerated, but as you move into a rhythm, you will feel a heightened sense of awareness. And as you breathe in and out slowly, you will relax your nervous system and busy mind. As you slowly walk through nature, take time to pick up a rock, or touch a tree or a flower. Take time to watch the birds or wildlife and note how they move in this environment. Notice how walking at this pace gives you a whole new perspective of life, compared to walking briskly. Notice how you feel at the end of your walk and take a moment to reflect on what you felt and saw during this time.

A meditation for balancing

Find a comfortable place to sit where your body is completely supported.

Close your eyes and use your breath to relax your body.

Ask yourself, 'What needs balance in my life?' You may need to slow down. You may need to eat healthier. Or perhaps you may need to step into your truth and have the courage to set boundaries with others.

Take note what thoughts come in about this. Allow it all to be here.

Now use your breath to breathe out what feels unbalanced in you. Breathe out any judgement you are holding about this imbalance and breathe it back into the earth.

We don't need to punish ourselves for being unbalanced, we need to nurture ourselves and create changes that will bring us back into alignment with life.

Now visualise yourself standing on the earth with your feet firmly planted on the ground. Imagine roots coming out of your feet and moving down into the many layers of the earth. Feel this strong foundation moving beneath your feet and grounding your energy.

Take some deep breaths in and out as you visualise this deep connection with Mother Earth.

Now visualise your body is the trunk of the tree and that your arms and your head are the branches expanding out of this tree. Take some deep breaths in and out as you lift your arms up, visualise this expanded energy moving in you and up into the sky.

Tune into your body and ask the question again. What needs balance in my life?

Spend some time now writing down your thoughts and intuition about this and what you can do to create change. Take some deep breaths in and out and finish when you are ready.

Final Thoughts

This year marks the twentieth anniversary of our son's death. At times, it feels surreal, knowing this much time has passed. Reflecting on these years has allowed me to see how much has transformed and expanded in me. It has given me a deep understanding that life is always moving, no matter what we are facing. It is only in hindsight that I can see the valuable wisdom and insights I have learned. It is only upon reflection that I can see the strength and resilience I have developed in stillness, and how this has led me to fulfilling my life's purpose.

It took many years for me to trust in life and to believe I would receive what I need. It took time to believe that the challenges I faced would eventually guide me into new spaces of renewal and healing. Looking back, I can remember the many times I was on my knees learning to surrender to 'what is'. And yet, here I am today, moving freely into the fullness and abundance of each moment, finally knowing I deserve this.

I now understand that it has been my daily practice that has opened my deepest sense of self and helped me explore and expand my gifts. My journey has uncovered what was hidden in me and awakened what is authentic. It took patience as I understood that I knew how to heal and how to move into the next moment.

Each time I faced my fears, my confidence expanded and allowed me to step out to do more. Each time I trusted my intuition, it led me to see the infinite possibilities in life. The more I understood myself and what I was capable of, the more I understood others and what they were capable of.

Change and movement are an inevitable part of our life. And yet, each of us has a choice to resist this momentum or to move with it and learn from it. Transformation and growth involve going beyond our comfort zones and trusting we can achieve so much more than we have been taught.

What I have learned is that I have control over three things in life: my thoughts, my response to life and my actions each day. It takes daily discipline to create a strong foundation in this truth, but this practice has never let me down. What I now know is that the sacrifice of facing death can be reborn into something beautiful.

Thank you for taking the time to read my story and for creating room to see life from a different perspective. May you discover the presence of the divine within you and find the courage to live from your truth.

I certainly don't have all the answers, and I still have so much to learn. But each time I stay present and flow with each moving moment, I become one with this beautiful and expansive life.

Namaste.

Karen Lang, 2021.

Acknowledgements

There were so many people who helped shape and create my book, and I am so grateful for their support.

Firstly, I would like to thank my beautiful family. To Michael, my partner of thirty-two years, thank you for being my rock throughout this deep and transformative journey. I could never have done this without you. To my divine daughters Lauren and April. To April who was the first person to suggest I write another book. To Lauren, who is always the first to read it, encouraging me to be creative and bold! You both inspire me, motivate me, challenge me, and I am so proud of you both and who you are becoming. To my parents, who are my biggest fans! Thank you for all your love and encouragement. To my sister Sheryl. Thank you for your generosity, support and love always. To my sister Lynn who has been by my side every step of the way. Thank you for your constant encouragement and for reminding me to believe in myself and to speak my truth. Thank you to my niece Laura for reading my book and encouraging me to keep going, it meant so much.

To Juliette Lachemeier, my amazing editor and managing director of The Erudite Pen. Thank you for challenging me to write from my heart. Thank you for structuring and bringing my book to life.

Thank you to my beautiful friends and extended family who always gave me words of encouragement. I am so grateful to each one of you.

Further Reading

Foor, Daniel, Ph.D. *Ancestral Medicine, Rituals for Personal and Family Healing*. New York: Simon and Schuster Publishing, 2017.

Lembo, Margaret Ann. *Chakra Awakening: Transform Your Reality Using Crystals, Color, Aromatherapy, and the Power of Positive Thought*. Woodbury: Llewellyn Worldwide, 2011.

Levine, Peter A. Ph.D. *Trauma and Memory: Brain and Body in a Search for the Living Past — A Practical Guide for Understanding and Working with Traumatic Memory*. California: North Atlantic Books, 2015.

Ober, Clinton, Sinatra, Stephen T., and Zucker, Martin, M.D. *Earthing: The Most Important Health Discovery Ever*. California: Basic Health Publications Inc., 2010.

Prechtel, Martin. *The Smell of Rain on Dust, Grief and Praise*. California: North Atlantic Books, 2015.

Tsabary, Shefali, Ph.D. *The Conscious Parent: Transforming Ourselves, Empowering Our Children*. Vancouver: Namaste Publishing, 2010.

Wagamese, Richard. *One Drum, Stories and Ceremonies for a Planet*. British Columbia: Douglas and McIntyre, 2019.

van Dernoot Lipsky, Laura, and Burk, Connie. *Trauma Stewardship: An Everyday Guide to Caring for Self While Caring for Others*. California: Berrett-Koehler Publishers Inc., 2009.

Notes

1. Karen Lang, *Courage: My journey through grief after the death of our child* (Queensland: Inhouse Publishing, 2016), 15.
2. Stephen Jenkinson, *Die Wise: A Manifesto for Sanity and Soul* (California: North Atlantic Books, 2015), 167.
3. Sadhguru, 'What is Surrender' Sadhguru Talks @ Meditator Sathsang, Isha Yoga Center, Coimbatore, Dec 2007, 2012. Video 8:39 https://www.youtube.com/watch?v=TMHhylNs-3Q
4. Kahlil Gibran, *The Prophet* (New York: Alfred A. Knopf Inc., 1973), 146.
5. Bhikkhu Analayo, *Satipatthana Meditation: A practice guide* (United Kingdom: Windhorse Publications, 2018), 144.
6. A. M. Mayer and Alexandra Poljakoff-Mayber, *The germination of seeds, third edition* (United Kingdom: Pergamon Press, 1982), 69.
7. Masuru Emoto, *The Hidden Messages of Water*, 3rd ed., trans. David A. Thayne (Oregon: Beyond Words Publishing Inc., 2001), 4.
8. Masuru Emoto, *The Hidden Messages of Water*, 3rd ed., trans. David A. Thayne (Oregon: Beyond Words Publishing Inc., 2001), 7.
9. Byron Katie with Stephen Mitchell, *Loving What Is* (New York: Random House, 2002), 29.
10. National Institute of Health, accessed April 11, 2021, https://www.nih.gov/health-information. Article: Craske MG, Stein MB. *Lancet*. 2016 Dec 17;388(10063):3048-3059. doi: 10.1016/S0140-6736(16)30381-6. Epub, 2016, Jun 24.
11. Claire Bidwell Smith, LCPC, *Anxiety: The missing stage of grief: A revolutionary approach to understanding and healing the impact of loss* (New York: Da Capo Press – Hachette Book Group, 2018) 7.
12. Dzogchen Ponlop Rinpoche, *Emotional rescue: How to work with your emotions to transform hurt and confusion into energy that empowers you* (New York: Penguin Random House, 2017), 91.
13. Shirley Riley, Forewords by Gerald D. Oster and Cathy A. Malchiodi *Contemporary Art Therapy with Adolescents* (London: Jessica Kingsley Publishers), 1999, 7, Paragraph 4.
    Earthing: Health Implications of Reconnecting the Human Body to the Earth's Surface Electrons
    Gaétan Chevalier, Stephen T. Sinatra, James L. Oschman, Karol Sokal, Pawel Sokal,
14. *J Environ Public Health*. 2012; 2012: 291541. Published online 2012 Jan 12. doi: 10.1155/2012/291541
15. Clint Oberman, Stephen T. Sinatra, M.D., and Martin Zucker, *Earthing: The Most Important Health Discovery Yet?* (California: Basic Health Publications, Inc., 2010), 6, paragraph 3.

16. Dan Hurley, https://www.discovermagazine.com/health/grandmas-experiences-leave-a-mark-on-your-genes, paragraph 10.
17. Patrick McGowan and Moshe Szyf, 'The epigenetics of social adversity in early life: Implications for Mental health outcomes,' *Journal in Neurobiology of Disease* 39, (2010): 66.
18. Dan Hurley, https://www.discovermagazine.com/health/grandmas-experiences-leave-a-mark-on-your-genes, paragraph 12.
19. "The Four Noble Truths," Knowledge-Buddhism, Nantien, accessed April 11, 2021, https://www.nantien.org.au/en/buddhism/knowledge-buddhism/four-noble-truths, Paragraph 20.
20. *Babel* is a 2006 psychological drama film directed by Alejandro González Iñárritu and written by Guillermo Arriaga.
21. Gary Chapman, *The 5 love languages: The secret to love that lasts, revised edition* (Chicago: Northfield Publishing, 2015), 3.
22. Jon Kabat-Zin, "Mindfulness Based Stress Reduction," Wikipedia, accessed April 9, 2021, https://en.wikipedia.org/wiki/Mindfulness-based_stress_reduction
23. Diane Coutu, "How Resilience Works," Organizational Structure, Harvard Business Review, accessed April 11, 2021, https://hbr.org/2002/05/how-resilience-works.
24. Babette Rothschild, *The Body Remembers*, (New York: W. W. Norton and Company, Inc., 2000), 37.
25. Peter A. Levine, PhD, *Trauma and Memory: Brain and body in a search for the living past* (California: North Atlantic Books, 2015), 7.
26. Erik Braun, *The birth of insight: Meditation, modern Buddhism, and the Burmese monk Ledi Sayadaw* (Chicago: The University of Chicago Press, 2013), 77.
27. C. G. Jung, *Dreams: Collected Works of C G Jung: Structure & Dynamics of the Psyche* (New Jersey: Princeton University Press, 2010), Page 16.
28. "Dreams," Wikipedia, accessed April 10, 2021, https://en.wikipedia.org/wiki/Dream.
29. Hans Christian Anderson, accessed April 9, 2021, https://www.goodreads.com/author/quotes/6378.Hans_Christian_Anderson
30. Joshua Fields and Ryan Nikodemus, *Minimalism: Live a meaningful life* (Montana: Asymmetrical Press, 2011), 10.
31. Stefan Stenudd, T*ao Quotes: The ancient wisdom of the Tao Te Ching by Lao Tzu* (Sweden: Arriba Malmo Publishing, 2015), 67.

ABOUT THE AUTHOR

Karen Lang's passion and purpose are to guide people out of their limiting stories and into their fullest potential. As a counsellor, energy healer and intuitive coach for over twelve years, she embraces the core values of understanding and empathy in her practice and guides her clients to heal deeply. She has spoken on grief at seminars and has run grief workshops for teenagers and adults.

She has a blog, *Living in this Moment*, which provides insights and inspiration for our daily lives. She is the author of two books, *Courage* and *Moving Moments*. Karen lives in Queensland, Australia, with her husband and two daughters.

Enjoyed the book? You can follow Karen Lang at:

Website: www.karenlangauthor.com

Blog: www.shamanismandhealing.wordpress.com

Instagram: www.instagram.com/k_langcounselling

www.ingramcontent.com/pod-product-compliance
Lightning Source LLC
Chambersburg PA
CBHW011147290426
44109CB00023B/2525